John Ireland Tucker

The SERVICE BOOK

John Ireland Tucker

The SERVICE BOOK

ISBN/EAN: 9783741123207

Manufactured in Europe, USA, Canada, Australia, Japa

Cover: Foto ©Angelika Wolter / pixelio.de

Manufactured and distributed by brebook publishing software (www.brebook.com)

John Ireland Tucker

The SERVICE BOOK

THE SERVICE BOOK;

A MANUAL OF

ANGLICAN CHANTS AND GREGORIAN TONES

ADAPTED TO THE CANTICLES;

WITH

MUSIC, OLD AND NEW, FOR THE SPECIAL OFFICES

OF THE

Book of Common Prayer.

NEW YORK:
F. J. HUNTINGTON AND CO., 107 DUANE STREET.
POTT, YOUNG AND CO., COOPER UNION.
MDCCCLXXV.

Entered, according to Act of Congress, in the year 1873, by
F. J. HUNTINGTON AND CO.,
In the Office of the Librarian of Congress, at Washington.

PREFACE.

This SERVICE BOOK is published with the wish of meeting the demands of many brethren who have introduced "THE HYMNAL, WITH TUNES OLD AND NEW," into their parishes. To adapt the Book to general use by fitting it to the tastes and preferences which may prevail in the several parishes, it contains English Chants with other Music, and Gregorian Tones for the Canticles and the Special Offices contained in the Book of Common Prayer. That I may not compromise myself, however, by this arrangement, I must express myself most positively in favour of the Gregorian Tones; and, after a long experience of Plain Song at the Church of the Holy Cross, I now most earnestly recommend the Gregorian Tones for Congregational use.

I would call particular attention to the Congregational *Te Deum* and *Gloria in Excelsis* written for this Book by MR. J. H. CORNELL, Organist of St. Paul's Chapel, New York, as good specimens of Churchlike musical composition.

To NATHAN B. WARREN, Esq., I am indebted for the permission to use portions of his *Communion Service*, which has been already published.

While the hearty co-operation of my friends, MR. ROUSSEAU and DR. WALTER, considerably lessens my Editorial labours, their efficient aid must necessarily take, as it deserves, much of the credit which kind friends have so generously attributed to my own efforts in the Service of Song. To DR. WALTER I must make special acknowledgments for the interest shown in my work by his patient industry, the skill and carefulness, and the willingness to carry out my wishes as far as practicable by a Church Musician, while supervising the publication of this Service Book.

J. IRELAND TUCKER.

PARSONAGE OF THE HOLY CROSS,
TROY, NEW YORK, CHRISTMAS DAY, 1872.

"Glory to God in the highest, and on earth peace, good-will toward men."

CHANTS.

Venite, exultemus Domino.

O come, let us **sing** | unto · the | Lord : ‖ let us heartily **rejôice** in the | strength · of | our · sal- | vation.

Let us come before His **présence** with | thanks- = | giving : ‖ and **show** ourselves | glad · in | Him · with | psalms.

For the **Lord** is a | great · = | God : ‖ and a great **King** a- | bove · = | all · = | gods.

In His hand are all the **côrners** | of · the | earth : ‖ and the **strength** of the | hills · is | His · = | also.

The sea is **His**, | and · He · | made it : ‖ and His **hands** pre- | par-ed the | dry · = | land.

O come, let us **wòrship**, | and · fall | down : ‖ and **kneel** be- | fore · the | Lord · our | Maker.

For **He** is the | Lord · our | God : ‖ and we are the people of His **pâsture**, and the | sheep · of | His · = | hand.

O worship the **Lord** in the | beauty · of | holiness : ‖ let the whole **earth** | stand · in | awe · of | Him.

For He cometh, for He **cômeth** to | judge · the | earth : ‖ and with righteousness to judge the **world**, and the | peo-ple | with · His | truth.

Glory be to the **Fâther**, | and · to the | Son : ‖ **and** | to · the | Ho-ly | Ghost ;

As it was in the beginning, is **now**, and | ev-er | shall be : ‖ **world** with- | out · end. | A- = | men.

Morning Prayer.

Venite, exultemus Domino.

O COME, let us **sing** | unto · the | Lord : ‖ let us heartily **rejoice** in the | strength · of | our · sal- | vation.

Let us come before His **presence** with | thanks- = | giving : ‖ and **show** ourselves | glad · in | Him · with | psalms.

For the **Lord** is a | great · = | God : ‖ and a great **King** a- | bove · = | all · = | gods.

In His hand are all the **corners** | of · the | earth : ‖ and the **strength** of the | hills · is | His · = | also.

The sea is **His**, | and · He · | made it : ‖ and His **hands** pre- | par-ed the | dry · = | land.

O come, let us **worship**, | and · fall | down : ‖ and **kneel** be- | fore · the | Lord · our | Maker.

For **He** is the | Lord · our | God : ‖ and we are the people of His **pasture**, and the | sheep · of | His · = | hand.

O worship the **Lord** in the | beauty · of | holiness : ‖ let the whole **earth** | stand · in | awe · of | Him.

For He cometh, for He **cometh** to | judge · the | earth : ‖ and with righteousness to judge the **world**, and the | peo-ple | with · His | truth.

Glory be to the **Father**, | and · to the | Son : ‖ **and** | to · the | Ho-ly | Ghost ;

As it was in the beginning, is **now**, and | ev-er | shall be : ‖ **world** with- | out · end. | A- = | men.

Morning Prayer.

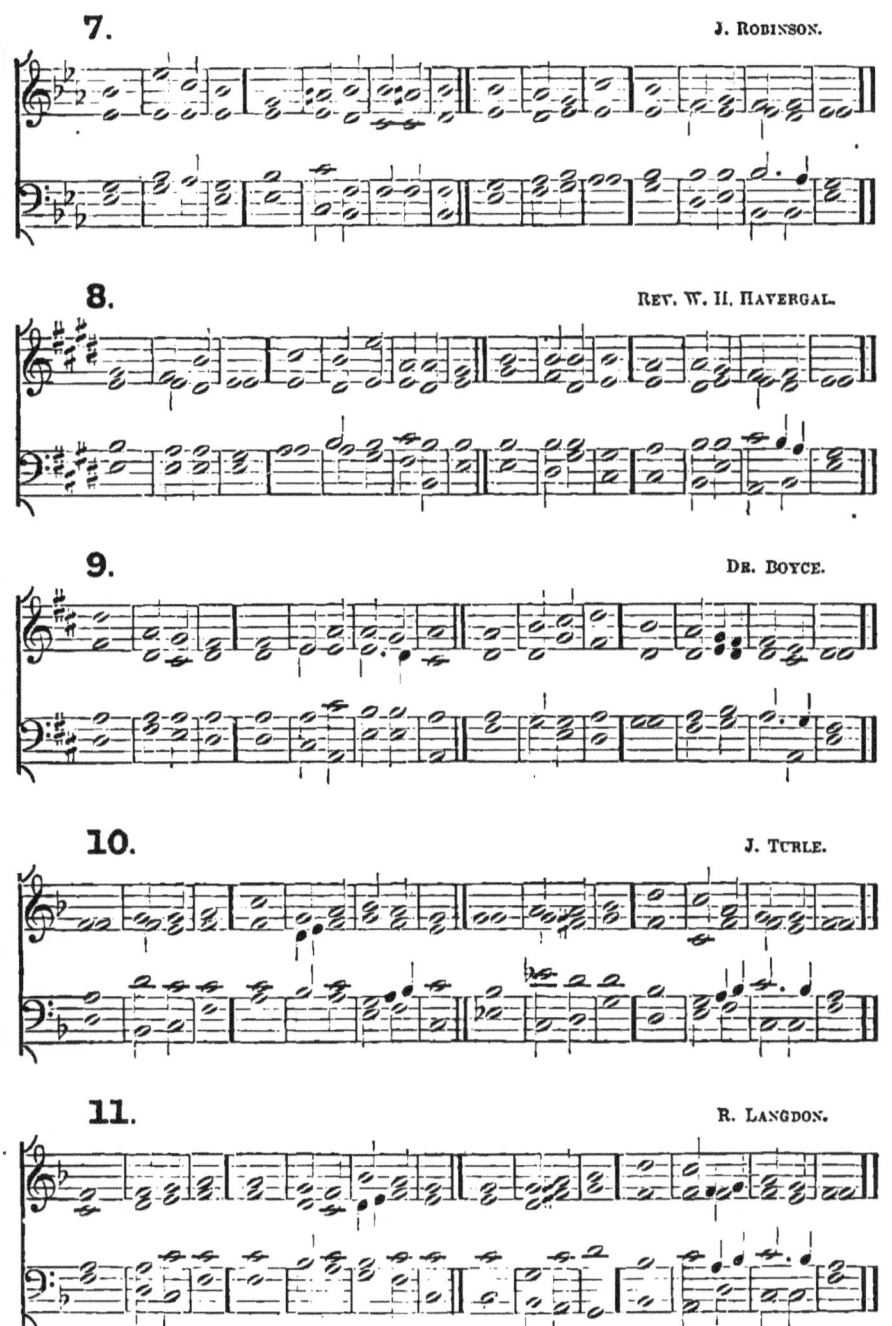

Morning Prayer.

12. GIBBONS.

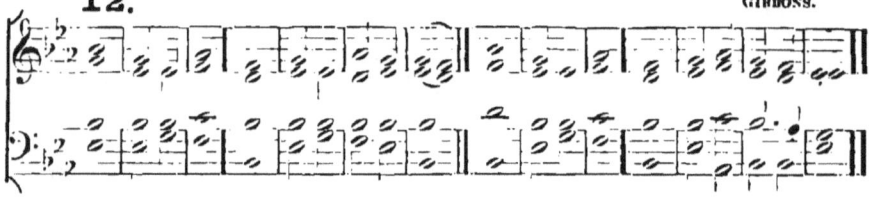

Te Deum laudamus.

FULL. We **praise** | Thee · O | God : ‖ we **acknowledge** | Thee · to | be · the | Lord.
All the **earth** doth | wor-ship | Thee : ‖ the **Father** | ev-er- | last = | ing.

DEC. To **Thee** all Angels | cry · a- | loud : ‖ the **Heavens**, and | all · the | powers · there- | in.

CAN. To **Thee**, Cherubim and | Se-raph- | im : ‖ **con-** | tin-ual- | ly · do | cry;

FULL. **Holy,** | Ho-ly, | Holy : ‖ **Lord** | God · of | Sa-ba- | oth ;
Heaven and | earth · are | full : ‖ of the | Majes-ty | of · Thy | glory.

DEC. The glorious company of the **Apostles** | praise · = | Thee : ‖

CAN. The goodly fellowship of the | Pro-phets | praise · = | Thee.

DEC. The noble army of **Martyrs** | praise · = | Thee : ‖

CAN. The holy Church throughout all the **world** | doth · ac | know-ledge | Thee ;

DEC. The **Father,** of an | in-finite | Majesty : ‖

CAN. Thine **adorable,** | true · and | on-ly | Son ;

DEC. **Also** the | Ho-ly | Ghost : ‖

CAN. **The** | Com = | = · fort- | er.

FULL. **Thou** | art · the | King : ‖ **of** | glo-ry, | O = | Christ.
Thou art the ever- | last-ing | Son : ‖ **of** | = · the | Fa · = | ther.

DEC. When Thou tookest upon **Thee** to de- | liv-er | man : ‖ Thou didst humble **Thyself** to be | born · = | of · a | Virgin.

CAN. When Thou hadst **overcome** the | sharpness · of | death : ‖ Thou didst open the **kingdom** of | Heaven · to | all · be- | lievers.

DEC. Thou sittest at the **right** | hand · of | God : ‖ **in** the | glo-ry | of · the | Father.

CAN. We **believe** that | Thou · shalt | come : ‖ **to** | be · = | our · = | Judge.

DEC. We therefore **pray** Thee | help · Thy | servants : ‖ whom Thou hast **redeemed** | with · Thy | pre-cious | blood.

CAN. Make them to be **numbered** | with · Thy | saints : ‖ in **glory** | ev-er- | last- · = | ing.

DEC. O **Lord,** | save · Thy | people : ‖ **and** | bless · Thine | her-it- | age.

CAN. **Gov-** · = · ern | them : ‖ **and** | lift · them | up · for | ever.

FULL. **Day** · = · by | day : ‖ **we** | mag-ni- | fy = | Thee ;
And we | worship · Thy | Name : ‖ **ever** | world · with- | out · | end.

DEC. **Vouch-** safe, O | Lord : ‖ to keep **us** | this · day | with-out | sin.

CAN. O **Lord,** have | mercy · up- | on us : ‖ **have** | mer-cy · up- | on · = | us.

FULL. O Lord, let Thy **mercy** be · up- | on us : ‖ **as** our | trust · | is · in | Thee.
O Lord, in **Thee** | have · I | trusted : ‖ **let** me | nev-er | be · con- | founded.

𝔐orning 𝔓rayer.

18.   FREDERICK HELMORE.

Te Deum laudamus.

FULL. *f* We **praise** Thee, O | God : we acknowledge **Thee** to | be · the | Lord.
   p All the earth doth **worship** | Thee : the **Father** ever- | *last-* | ing.
DEC.   To **Thee** all Angels cry a- | loud : the Heavens and **all** the | powers · there- | in.
CAN.   To **Thee** Cherubim and Sera- | phim : **continual-** | ly · do | cry,
FULL. *p* Holy, Holy, | Holy : Lord **God** of | Sa‑ba‑ | oth ;
   f Heaven and earth are **full** of the | Majesty : of Thy | *glo-* | ry.
            FULL.
DEC.   The glorious **company** of the A- | postles : praise | = = | Thee.
            FULL.
CAN.   The goodly **fellowship** of the | Prophets : praise | = = | Thee.
            FULL.
DEC.   The noble **army** of | Martyrs : praise | = = | Thee.
CAN.   The holy **Church** throughout all the | world : **doth** ac- | know-ledge | Thee ;
DEC.   The | Father : of an infinite | Ma‑jes‑ | ty.
CAN.   Thine **adorable,** | true : and | on‑ly | Son ;
                       p
DEC.   Also the Holy | Ghost : the | Com‑fort‑ | er.

FULL. } **Thou** art the King of | glory : O | = = | Christ.
unison.
FULL. } **Thou** art the everlasting | Son : **of** the | *Fa-* | ther.
unison.
CAN. *p* When Thou tookest upon Thee to deliver | man : Thou didst humble thyself to be **born** | of · a | Virgin.
       cres.   *p*
DEC.   When Thou hadst overcome the **sharpness** of | death : Thou didst open the kingdom of Heaven to **all** be- | *liev-* | ers.
CAN. *f* Thou sittest at the right **hand** of | God : in the **glory** of the | *Fa-* | ther.

Morning Prayer.

CAN. *p* We therefore **pray** Thee, help Thy | servants : whom Thou hast **redêemed** with Thy | pre - cious | blood.
DEC. *cres.* Make them to be **númbered** with Thy | Saints : in **glôry** ever - | last- | ing.
CAN. *p* O Lord, **save** Thy | people : and **bless** Thine | her - i - | tage.
DEC. **Gôvern** | them : and **lift** them | up · for | ever.
FULL. *f* **Day** by | day : we magni - | fy = | Thee.
FULL. *p* And we **wôrship** Thy | Name : **êver** | world with-out | end.
CAN. *p* **Vouchsâfe**, O | Lord : to keep us this day | with - out | sin.
DEC. *p* O Lord, have **mêrcy** up- | on us : have | mercy · up- | on us.
CAN. O Lord, let Thy mercy be up- | on us : as our **trust** | is · in | Thee.

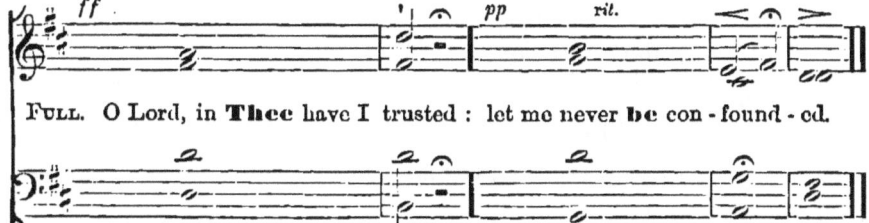

FULL. O Lord, in **Thee** have I trusted : let me never **be** con - found - ed.

Te Deum laudamus.

FULL. We | praise · Thee, | 'O · = | God : ‖ we **acknowledge** | Thee · to | be · = | the⌒Lord.
All the | earth · doth | wor- · = | ship⌒Thee : ‖ the **Father** | ev - er- | last- · = | ing.

DEC. To **Thee** all | 'An-gels | cry · = | aloud : ‖ the **Heavens**, and | all · the | powers · = | therein.

CAN. To **Thee**, Cheru- | bim · and | Se- · = | raphim : ‖ con- | tin - ual- | ly · = | do⌒cry,

FULL. **Holy,** | Ho-ly, | Ho- · = | ly : ‖ **Lord** | God · of | Sa- = | baoth ;
Heaven and **earth** are | full · of⌒the | Ma- · = | jesty : ‖ **of** | Thy · = | glo- · = | ry.

DEC. The glorious **company** of the A- | pos - tles | praise · = | Thee : ‖

CAN. The goodly **fellowship** of the | Pro- phets | praise · = | Thee.

DEC. The noble **army** of | Mar - tyrs | praise · = | Thee : ‖

CAN. The holy Church throughout all the **world** | doth · ac- | know- · = | ledge Thee ;

DEC. The **Father** of an | in - finite | Ma- · = | jesty : ‖ Thine **adorable,** | true · and | on- · = | ly⌒Son ;

CAN. Al- | so · the | Ho- · = | ly Ghost : ‖ **the** | Com- · = | '= · = | forter.

FULL. Thou art the **King** of | glo-ry, | 'O · = | Christ : ‖ Thou art the ever-lasting **Son** | of · the | Fa- · = | ther.

DEC. When Thou tookest upon **Thee** | to · de- | liv- · = | er⌒man : ‖ Thou didst humble **Thyself** to be | born · of a | Vir- · = | gin.

CAN. When Thou hadst **overcome** the | sharp-ness | of · = | death : ‖ Thou didst open the **kingdom** of | Heaven · to | all · be- | lievers.

DEC. Thou **sittest** | at⌒the · right | hand · = | of⌒God : ‖ in the **glory** | of · the | Fa- · = | ther.

CAN. We be- | lieve · that | Thou · = | shalt⌒come : ‖ **to** | be · = | our · = | Judge.

DEC. We therefore **pray** Thee, | help · Thy | ser- = | vants : ‖ whom Thou hast **redeemed** | with · Thy | pre- · = | cious⌒blood.

CAN. Make them to be **numbered** | with · = | Thy · = | Saints : ‖ in **glory** ev - er - | last- = | ing.

DEC. O Lord, save Thy **people,** and | bless · Thine | her- = | itage : ‖ Govern **them,** and | lift · them | up · for | ever.

FULL. **Day** by | day · we | magni-fy | Thee : ‖ and we worship Thy **Name** | ev - er, | world⌒with-out | end.

CAN. **Vouch-** | safe, = | 'O · = | Lord : ‖ to **keep** us | this · day⌒with- | out · — | sin.

DEC. O **Lord,** have | mer-cy⌒up- | on · = | us : ‖ **have** | mer-cy⌒up- | on · — | us.

CAN. O Lord, let Thy **mercy** | be · up- | on · = | us : ‖ **as** our | trust · is | in · = | Thee.

FULL. O Lord, in **Thee** | have · I | trust- = | ed : ‖ let me **never** | be · con- | found- = | ed.

Te Deum laudamus.

Morning Prayer.

Benedicite, omnia opera Domini.

O ALL ye works of the **Lord**, | bless · ye the | Lord : ‖ praise **Him**, and | magni-fy | Him · for | ever.

O ye Angels of the **Lord**, | bless · ye the | Lord : ‖ praise **Him**, and | magni-fy | Him · for | ever.

O ye **Heavens**, | bless · ye the | Lord : ‖ praise **Him**, and | magni-fy | Him · for | ever.

O ye Waters that be above the **Firmament**, | bless · ye the | Lord : ‖ praise **Him**, and | magni-fy | Him · for | ever.

O all ye Powers of the **Lord**, | bless · ye the | Lord : ‖ praise **Him**, and | magni-fy | Him · for | ever.

O ye Sun and **Moon**, | bless · ye the | Lord : ‖ praise **Him**, and | magni-fy | Him · for | ever.

O ye Stars of **Heaven**, | bless · ye the | Lord : ‖ praise **Him**, and | magni-fy | Him · for | ever.

O ye Showers and **Dew**, | bless · ye the | Lord : ‖ praise **Him**, and | magni-fy | Him · for | ever.

O ye Winds of **God**, | bless · ye the | Lord : ‖ praise **Him**, and | magni-fy | Him · for | ever.

O ye Fire and **Heat**, | bless · ye the | Lord : ‖ praise **Him**, and | magni-fy | Him · for | ever.

Morning Prayer. 17

O ye Winter and **Summer**, | bless · ye the | Lord : ‖ praise **Him**, and | magni-fy | Him · for | ever.
O ye Dews and **Frosts**, | bless · ye the | Lord : ‖ praise **Him**, and | magni-fy | Him · for | ever.
O ye Frost and **Cold**, | bless · ye the | Lord : ‖ praise **Him**, and | magni-fy | Him · for | ever.
O ye Ice and **Snow**, | bless · ye the | Lord : ‖ praise **Him**, and | magni-fy | Him · for | ever.
O ye Nights and **Days**, | bless · ye the | Lord : ‖ praise **Him**, and | magni-fy | Him · for | ever.
O ye Light and **Darkness**, | bless · ye the | Lord : ‖ praise **Him**, and | magni-fy | Him · for | ever.
O ye Lightnings and **Clouds**, | bless · ye the | Lord : ‖ praise **Him**, and | magni-fy | Him · for | ever.
O let the **Earth**, | bless · — the | Lord : ‖ **Yea**, let it praise **Him**, and | magni-fy | Him · for | ever.
O ye Mountains and **Hills**, | bless · ye the | Lord : ‖ praise **Him**, and | magni-fy | Him · for | ever.
O all ye Green Things upon the **Earth**, | bless · ye the | Lord : ‖ praise **Him**, and | magni-fy | Him · for | ever.
O ye **Wells**, | bless · ye the | Lord : ‖ praise **Him**, and | magni-fy | Him · for | ever.
O ye Seas and **Floods**, | bless · ye the | Lord : ‖ praise **Him**, and | magni-fy | Him · for | ever.
O ye **Whales**, and all that move in the **waters**, | bless · ye the | Lord : ‖ praise **Him**, and | magni-fy | Him · for | ever.
O all ye Fowls of the **Air**, | bless · ye the | Lord : ‖ praise **Him**, and | magni-fy | Him · for | ever.
O all ye Beasts and **Cattle**, | bless · ye the | Lord : ‖ praise **Him**, and | magni-fy | Him · for | ever.
O ye children of **Men**, | bless · ye the Lord : ‖ praise **Him**, and | magni-fy | Him · for | ever.
O let **Israel** | bless · — the | Lord : ‖ praise **Him**, and | magni-fy | Him · for | ever.
O ye Priests of the **Lord**, | bless · ye the | Lord : ‖ praise **Him**, and | magni-fy | Him · for | ever.
O ye Servants of the **Lord**, | bless · ye the | Lord : ‖ praise **Him**, and | magni-fy | Him · for | ever.
O ye Spirits and Souls of the **Righteous**, | bless · ye the | Lord : ‖ praise **Him**, and | magni-fy | Him · for | ever.
O ye holy and humble Men of **Heart**, | bless · ye the | Lord : ‖ praise **Him**, and | magni-fy | Him · for | ever.
Glory be to the **Father**, | and · to the Son : ‖ **and** | to · the | Ho-ly | Ghost. ·
As it was in the beginning, is **now**, and | ev - er | shall be : ‖ **world** with- | out · end. | A- — | men.

Morning Prayer.

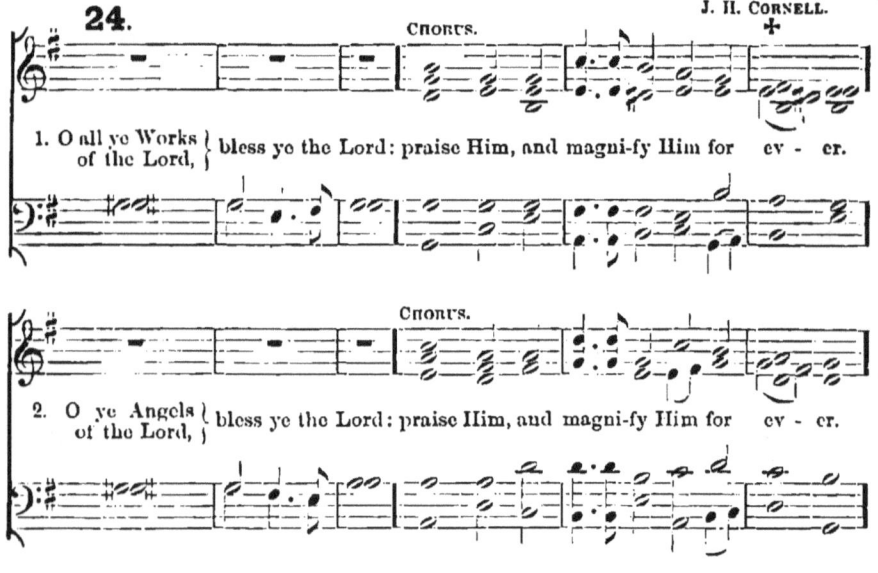

24. J. H. Cornell.

1. O all ye Works of the Lord, bless ye the Lord: praise Him, and magni-fy Him for ev-er.

2. O ye Angels of the Lord, bless ye the Lord: praise Him, and magni-fy Him for ev-er.

Benedicite, omnia opera Domini.

O ALL ye Works of the **Lord,** | bless · ye the | Lord : ‖ praise Him, and | magni-fy | Him · for | ev-er.

O ye Angels of the **Lord,** | bless · ye the | Lord : ‖ praise Him, and | magni-fy | Him · for | ev-er.

O ye **Heavens,** | bless · ye the | Lord : ‖ praise Him, &c.

O ye Waters that be above the **Firmament,** | bless · ye the | Lord : ‖ praise Him, &c.

O all ye Powers of the **Lord,** | bless · ye the | Lord : ‖ praise Him, &c.

O ye Sun and **Moon,** | bless · ye the | Lord : ‖ praise Him, &c.

O ye Stars of **Heaven,** | bless · ye the | Lord : ‖ praise Him, &c.

O ye Showers and **Dew,** | bless · ye the | Lord : ‖ praise Him, &c.

O ye Winds of **God,** | bless · ye the | Lord : ‖ praise Him, &c.

O ye Fire and **Heat,** | bless · ye the | Lord : ‖ praise Him, &c.

O ye Winter and **Summer,** | bless · ye the | Lord : ‖ praise Him, &c.

O ye Dews and **Frosts,** | bless · ye the | Lord : ‖ praise Him, &c.

O ye Frost and **Cold,** | bless · ye the | Lord : ‖ praise Him, &c.

O ye Ice and **Snow,** | bless · ye the | Lord : ‖ praise Him, &c.

O ye Nights and **Days,** | bless · ye the | Lord : ‖ praise Him, &c.

O ye Light and **Darkness,** | bless · ye the | Lord : ‖ praise Him, &c.

O ye Lightnings and **Clouds,** | bless · ye the | Lord : ‖ praise Him, &c.

O **let** the | Earth · bless the | Lord : ‖ Yea, let it **praise** Him, and | magni-fy | Him · for | ev-er.

Morning Prayer. 19

O ye Mountains and **Hills**, | bless · ye the | Lord : || praise Him, &c.
O all ye Green Things upon the **Earth**, | bless · ye the | Lord : || praise Him, &c.
O ye **Wells**, | bless · ye the | Lord : || praise Him, &c.
O ye Seas and **Floods**, | bless · ye the | Lord : || praise Him, &c.
O ye **Whales**, and all that move in the **waters**, | bless · ye the | Lord : || praise Him, &c.
O all ye Fowls of the **Air**, | bless · ye the | Lord : || praise Him, &c.
O all ye Beasts and **Cattle**, | bless · ye the | Lord : || praise Him, &c.
O ye children of **Men**, | bless · ye the | Lord : || praise Him, &c.
O let **Isra-** | el · bless the | Lord : || praise Him, &c.
O ye Priests of the **Lord**, | bless · ye the | Lord : || praise Him, &c.
O ye Servants of the **Lord**, | bless · ye the | Lord : || praise Him, &c.
O ye Spirits and Souls of the **Righteous**, | bless · ye the | Lord : || praise Him, &c.
O ye holy and humble Men of **Heart**, | bless · ye the | Lord : || praise Him, &c.

Morning Prayer.

Jubilate Deo.
Psalm c.

O be joyful in the **Lord**, | all · ye | lands : ‖ serve the Lord with gladness, and **come** before His | pre-sence | with · a | song.

Be ye sure that the **Lord**, | He · is | God : ‖ it is He that hath made us, and not we ourselves; we are His **people**, and the | sheep · of | His = | pasture.

O go your way into His gates with thanksgiving, and into His **courts** | with =| praise : ‖ be thankful unto **Him**, and | speak · good | of · His | Name.

For the Lord is gracious, His **mercy** is | ev - er - | lasting : ‖ and His truth endureth from **generâtion** to | gen - er - | a - = | tion.

Glo-ry be to the **Fâther**, | and · to the | Son : ‖ **and** | to · the | Ho-ly | Ghost ; As it was in the beginning, is **now**, and | ev - er | shall be : ‖ **world** with-| out · end. | A- = | men.

Morning Prayer.

Morning Prayer. 23

Benedictus.
St. Luke i. 68.

BLESSED be the Lord **God** of | Is - ra- | el : ‖ for He hath **visited,** | and · re- | deemed · His | people ;

And hath raised up a mighty **salvation** | for · = | us : ‖ in the **house** | of · His | ser - vant | David ;

As he spake by the **mouth** of His | ho - ly | Prophets : ‖ which have **been** | since · the | world · be- | gan ;

That we should be **saved** | from · our | enemies : ‖ and from the **hand** of | all · that | hate · = | us ;

GLO-RY be to the **Father,** | and · to the | Son : ‖ **and** | to · the | Ho-ly | Ghost ;

As it was in the beginning, is **now,** and | ev - er | shall be : ‖ **world** with-| out · end. | A- = | men.

Evening Prayer.

48. Dr. Randall.
49. Lord Mornington.
50. T. Attwood.

Cantate Domino.
Psalm xcviii.

O sing unto the **Lord** a | new · = | song : ‖ for **He** | hath · done | mar- vellous | things.
With His own right **hand**, and with His | ho - ly | arm : ‖ hath He **gôtten** Him- | self · the | vic - to- | ry.
The Lord **declâred** | His · sal- | va - tion : ‖ His righteousness hath He openly **shôwed** in the | sight · of the | hea- = | then.
He hath remembered His mercy and truth toward the | house of | Is - ra- | el : ‖ and all the ends of the world have **seen** the sal- | va - tion | of · our | God.
Show yourselves joyful unto the **Lord**, | all · ye | lands : ‖ **sing**, re- | joice, and | give · = | thanks.
Praise the **Lord** up- | on · the | harp : ‖ sing to the **harp** with a | psalm · of | thanks- = | giving.
With **trûmpets** | also · and | shawms : ‖ O show yourselves **jôyful** be- | fore · the | Lord, · the | King.
Let the sea make a noise, and **all** that | there - in | is : ‖ the round **world**, and | they · that | dwell · there- | in.
Let the floods clap their hands, and let the hills be joyful **togêther** be- | fore · the | Lord : ‖ for **He** | cometh · to | judge · the | earth.
With righteousness **shall** He | judge · the | world : ‖ **and** the | peo - ple with | e - qui - | ty.
Glory be to the **Fâther**, | and · to the | Son : ‖ **and** ! to · the | Ho-ly | Ghost.
As it was in the beginning, is **now**, and | ev - er | shall be : ‖ **world** with- | out · end. | A- = | men.

Evening Prayer.

Bonum est confiteri.
Psalm xcii.

It is a good thing to give **thanks** | unto · the | Lord : ‖ and to sing praises unto Thy **Name**, | O · = | Most · = | Highest.

To tell of Thy loving-kindness **êarly** | in · the | morning : ‖ and of Thy **truth** | in · the | night · = | season.

Upon an instrument of ten **strings**, and up- | on · the | lute : ‖ upon a loud **instrument**, | and · up- | on · the | harp.

For Thou, Lord, hast made me **glad** | through · Thy | works : ‖ and I will rejoice in giving **praise** for the oper- | a - tions | of · Thy | hands.

Glo-ry be to the **Fáther**, | and · to the | Son : ‖ **and** | to · the | Ho-ly | Ghost ;

As it was in the beginning, is **now**, and | ev - er | shall be : ‖ **world** with- | out · end. | A- = | men.

Evening Prayer.

Evening Prayer.

65. J. H. CORNELL.

66. W. HAWES.

67. T. ATTWOOD.

Deus misereatur.
Psalm lxvii.

God be merciful unto **us**, and | bless · = | us : ‖ and show us the light of His countenance, **and** be | merci - ful | un - to | us;

That Thy **way** may be | known up - on | earth : ‖ Thy saving **health** a - | mong · = | all · = | nations.

Let the people **praise** | Thee, · O | God : ‖ yea, let **all** the | peo - ple | praise · = | Thee.

O let the nations **rejoice**, | and · be | glad : ‖ for Thou shalt judge the folk righteously, and **govern** the | na - tions up- | on · = | earth.

Let the people **praise** | Thee, · O | God : ‖ yea, let **all** the | peo - ple | praise · = | Thee.

Then shall the **earth** bring | forth · her | increase : ‖ and God, even our own **God**, shall | give · us | His · = | blessing.

God shall | bless · = | us : ‖ and all the ends of the **world** | shall · = | fear · = | Him.

Glory be to the **Father,** | and · to the | Son : ‖ **and** | to · the | Ho - ly | Ghost;

As it was in the beginning, is **now**, and | ev - er | shall be : ‖ **world** with- | out · end. | A- = | men.

Evening Prayer. 31

73. Dr. Barrow.

74. T. Norris.

75. Dr. B. Cooke.

Benedic, anima mea.

Psalm ciii.

Praise the Lord, | O · my | soul : ‖ and all that is **within** me | praise · His | ho - ly | Name.

Praise the **Lord**, | O · my | soul : ‖ and forget **not** | all · His | ben - e - | fits ;

Who **forgiveth** | all · thy | sin : ‖ and healeth **all** | thine · in- | firm - i - | ties;

Who saveth thy **life** | from · de- | struction : ‖ and crowneth thee with **mercy** and | lov - ing - | kind- = | ness.

O praise the Lord, ye Angels of His, **ye** that ex- | cel · in | strength : ‖ ye that fulfil His commandment, and **hearken** unto the | voice · of | His · = | word.

O praise the **Lord**, all | ye · His | hosts : ‖ ye **servants** of | His · that | do · His | pleasure.

O speak good of the Lord, all ye works of His, in all **places** of | His · do- | minion : ‖ praise thou the **Lord**, | O · = | my · = | soul.

Glory be to the **Father**, | and · to the | Son : ‖ **and** ! to · the | Ho-ly | Ghost;

As it was in the beginning, is **now**, and | ev - er | shall be : ‖ **world** with- | out · end. | A- = | men.

E

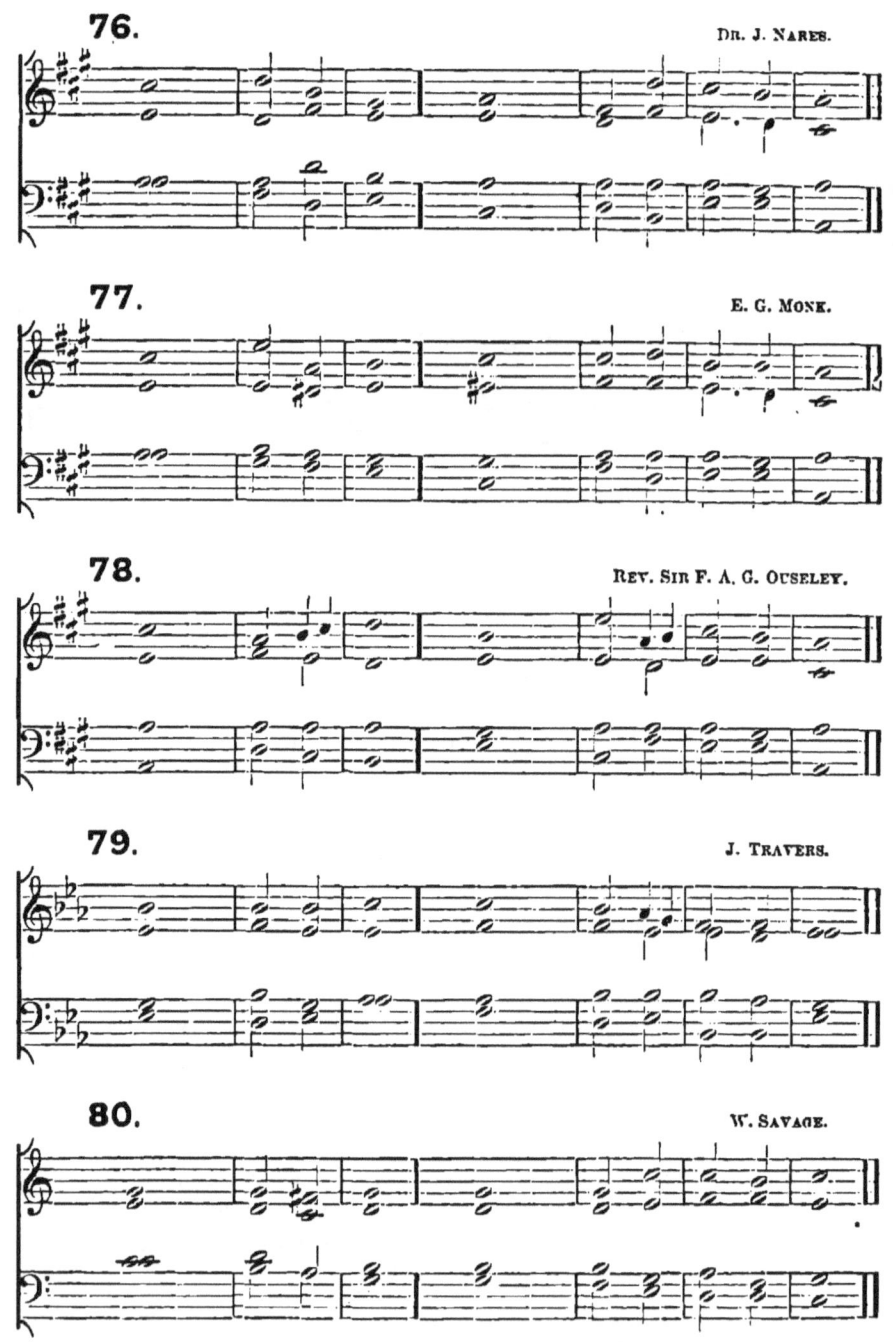

Easter Day.

Instead of "O come, let us sing," &c.

CHRIST our Passover is **sacrificed** | for · = | us : ‖ **therefore** | let · us | keep · the | feast ;
Not with the old leaven, neither with the **leaven** of | malice · and | wickedness : ‖ but with the unleavened **bread** of sin- | cer - i - | ty · and | truth. 1 *Cor.* v. 7.

CHRIST being raised from the **dead,** | dieth · no | more : ‖ death hath no **more** do- | min - ion | o - ver | Him.
For in that He died, He **died** unto | sin · = | once : ‖ but in that He **liveth,** He | liv - eth | un - to | God.
Likewise reckon ye also yourselves to be dead **indeed** | un - to | sin : ‖ but alive unto **God** through | Je - sus | Christ · our | Lord. *Rom.* vi. 9.

CHRIST is **risen** | from · the | dead : ‖ and become the **first-fruits** | of · = | them · that | slept.
For **since** by | man · came | death : ‖ by man came **also** the resur- | rec - tion | of · the | dead.
For as in **Adam** | all · = | die : ‖ even so in **Christ** shall | all · be | made · a- | live. 1 *Cor.* xv. 20.

GLO-RY be to the **Father,** | and · to the | Son : ‖ **and** | to · the | Ho-ly | Ghost ;
As it was in the beginning, is **now,** and | ev - er | shall be : ‖ **world** with- | out · end. | A- = | men.

84. Dr. W. Hayes.

85. Dr. Rimbault.

86. Rev. Sir F. A. G. Ouseley.

Laudate Dominum.

Instead of "O come, let us sing," &c.

Praise ye the Lord; for it is good to sing **praises** | unto · our | God : ‖ **for** it is ᛁ pleasant · and | praise · is | comely.

The Lord doth **build up** Je- | ru-sa- | lem : ‖ He gathereth **together** the | out - casts of | Is - ra - ᛁ el.

He healeth **those** that are | broken · in | heart : ‖ **and** | bind - eth | up · their | wounds.

He covereth the heaven with clouds, and **prepareth** | rain · for the | earth : ‖ He maketh the **grass** to | grow · up - | on · the | mountains.

He **giveth** to the | beast · his | food : ‖ **and** to the | young · = | ravens · which | cry.

Praise the **Lord**, | O · Je- | rusalem : ‖ praise thy **God**, | O · = | Si - = | on.

For He hath strengthened the **bars** | of · thy | gates : ‖ He hath **blessed** thy | child - ren with - | in = | thee.

He maketh **peace** | in · thy | borders : ‖ and filleth **thee** with the | fi - nest | of · the | wheat.

Glory be to the **Father**, | and · to the | Son : ‖ **and** | to · the | Ho-ly | Ghost;

As it was in the beginning, is **now**, and | ev - er | shall be : ‖ **world** with- | out · end. | A - = | men.

Institution of Ministers.

87. — T. PURCELL.

88. — DR. ALCOCK.

Laudate Nomen.

O **praise** the Lord, laud ye the **Name** | of · the | Lord : ‖ praise it, O ye | servants | of · the | Lord.

Ye that stand in the **house** | of · the | Lord : ‖ in the **courts** of the | house · of | our · = | God.

O praise the **Lord**, for the | Lord · is | gracious : ‖ O sing **praises** unto His | Name, · for | it · is | lovely.

The Lord is **gracious**, and | mer - ci - | ful : ‖ **long** - suffering, | and · of | great · = | goodness.

The Lord is **loving** unto | eve - ry | man : ‖ and His **mercy** is | o - ver | all · His | works.

All Thy works **praise** | Thee, · O | Lord : ‖ **and** Thy | saints · give | thanks · unto | Thee.

The Lord doth **build up** | Je - ru - | sa - lem : ‖ and gather **together** the | out - casts of | Is - ra - | el.

He healeth **those** that are | broken · in | heart : ‖ and giveth **medicine** to | heal · = | their · = | sickness.

The Lord's delight is in **them** that | fear · = | Him : ‖ and put their **trust** | in · = | His · = | mercy.

Praise the **Lord**, | O - Je - | rusalem : ‖ praise thy **God**, | O · = | Si - = | on.

For He hath made fast the **bars** | of · thy | gates : ‖ and hath **blessed** Thy | child - ren with - | in · = | Thee.

He maketh **peace** | in · thy | borders : ‖ and filleth **thee** | with · the | flour · of | wheat.

He is our God, even the **God** of whom | cometh · sal - | vation : ‖ God is the **Lord** by | whom · we es - | cape · = | death.

O God, wonderful art **Thou** in Thy | ho - ly | places : ‖ even the God of Israel, He will give strength and power unto His **people**. | Bless - ed | be · = | God.

Glory be to the **Father**, | and · to the | Son : ‖ **and** | to · the | Ho - ly | Ghost;

As it was in the beginning, is **now**, and | ev - er | shall be : ‖ **world** with - | out · end. | A - = | men.

Consecration of Churches.

89. FARRANT.

90. P. HUMPHREY.

91. OLD SCOTCH CHANT.

Domini est terra.
Psalm xxiv.

The earth is the Lord's, and **all** that | there-in | is : ‖ the compass of the **world**, and | they · that | dwell · there - | in.

For He hath founded **it** up- | on · the | seas : ‖ and **prepared** | it · up- | on · the | floods.

Who shall ascend into the **hill** | of · the | Lord : ‖ or who shall rise **up** | in · His | ho-ly | place ?

Even he that hath clean **hands** and a | pure · = | heart : ‖ and that hath not lift up his mind unto vanity, nor **sworn** | to · de - | ceive · his | neighbour.

He shall receive the **blessing** | from · the | Lord : ‖ and righteousness **from** the | God · of | his · sal - | vation.

This is the generation of **them** that | seek · = | Him : ‖ even of **them** that | seek · thy | face, · O | Jacob.

Lift up your heads, O ye gates ; and be ye lift **up**, ye ever-| last - ing | doors : ‖ and the **King** of | glo-ry | shall · come | in.

Who **is** the | King · of | glory : ‖ It is the Lord strong and mighty, **even** the | Lord · = | mighty · in | battle.

Lift up your heads, O ye gates ; and be ye lift **up**, ye ever-| last - ing | doors : ‖ and the **King** of | glo - ry | shall · come | in.

Who **is** the | King · of | glory : ‖ Even the Lord of **hosts**, | He · is the | King · of | glory.

GLO RY be to the **Father**, | and · to the | Son : ‖ **and** | to · the | Ho-ly | Ghost ;

As it was in the beginning, is **now**, and | ev - er | shall be : ‖ **world** with- | out · end. | A- = | men.

Occasional Anthems. 37

92.
J. H. CORNELL.

1st v. *Soprano or Tenor Solo*; 2d v. *Chorus, and so on, alternately.*

Miserere mei, Deus.
From Psalm li.

HAVE mercy upon me, O **God**, after | Thy · great | good- = | ness : ‖ according to the multitude of Thy mercies **do** a- | way · = | mine · of- | fen- = | ces.

Wash me **thrôughly** | from · my | wick - ed - | ness : ‖ **and** | cleanse · = | me · = | from · my | sin.

For **I** ac- | know - ledge | my · = | faults : ‖ **and** my | sin · is | ever · be - | fore · = | me.

Against Thee only have **I** sinned, and **done** this | evil · in | Thy · = | sight : ‖ that Thou mightest be justified in Thy **sáying**, and | clear · when | Thou · art | judg- = | ed.

Behôld, I was | shapen · in | wick - ed - | ness : ‖ and | in sin | hath · my | mother · con- | ceiv-ed | me.

But lo, Thou **requirest** | truth · in the | in - ward | parts : ‖ and shalt make **me** to | under-stand | wis-dom | se-cret- | ly.

Thou shalt purge me with **hýssop**, | and · **I** | shall · be | clean : ‖ Thou shalt wash me, **and I** | shall · be | whi-ter | than · = | snow.

Thou shalt make me **hear** of | joy · and | glad- = | ness : ‖ that the **bones** which | Thou · hast | bro-ken | may · re- | joice.

Turn Thy | face · from | my · = | sins : ‖ **and** | put · out | all · = | my · mis- | deeds.

Make **me** a | clean · heart, | O · = | God : ‖ and | **renêw** a | right · = | spirit · with- | in · = | me.

Cast me not **awây** | from · Thy | pre- = | sence : ‖ and take **not** Thy | Ho-ly | Spir-it | from · = | me.

O give me the **cômfort** | of · Thy | help · a- | gain : ‖ and | **stâblish** | me · with | Thy · = | free · = | Spirit.

Then shall I **teach** Thy | ways · un- | to · the | wicked : ‖ and | **sinners** shall | be · con- | vert-ed | un-to | Thee.

Deliver me from blood-guiltiness, O God, Thou that **art** the | God · of | my · = | health : ‖ **and** my | tongue · shall | sing of · Thy | right-eous- | ness.

Thou shalt | open · my | lips, · O | Lord : ‖ **and** my | mouth · shall | show · = | Thy · = | praise.

For Thou desirest no **sâcrifice**, | else · would I | give · it | Thee : ‖ but **Thou** de- | light-est | not · in | burnt- = | offerings.

The sacrifice of **God** | is · a | trou - bled | spirit : ‖ a broken and contrite **heart**, O | God, · shalt | Thou · = | not · de- | spise.

Glory **be** to the | Fa-ther, | and · to the | Son : ‖ **and** | to · the | Ho- = | = · ly | Ghost ;

As it was in the beginning, is **now**, and | ev-er | shall · = | be : ‖ **world** with- | out · end. | A- = | = · = | men.

Occasional Anthems.

93. Rev. W. Felton.

94. Dr. Crotch.

95. Farrant.

Burial of the Dead.

Lord, let me know my end, and the **number** | of · my | days : ‖ that I may be **certified** how | long · I | have · to | live.

Behold, Thou hast made my days as it **were** a | span · = | long : ‖ and mine age is even as nothing in respect of Thee; and verily every man **living** is | al - to- | geth - er | vanity.

For man walketh in a vain shadow, and **disquieteth** him- | self · in | vain : ‖ he heapeth up riches, and cannot **tell** | who · shall | gath - er | them.

And now, **Lord**, | what is · my | hope : ‖ **Truly** my | hope · is | even · in | Thee.

Deliver me from **all** | mine · of - | fences : ‖ and make me **not** a re- | buke · un- | to · the | foolish.

When Thou with rebukes dost chasten man for sin, Thou makest his beauty to consume away, like as it were a **moth** | fretting · a | garment : ‖ every **man** | there - fore | is · but | vanity.

Hear my prayer, O Lord, and with Thine **ears** con- | sider · my | calling : ‖ hold **not** Thy | peace · = | at · my | tears;

For I **am** a | stranger · with | Thee : ‖ and a **sojourner** as | all · my | fathers | were.

O spare me a little, that I **may** re- | cover · my | strength : ‖ before I go **hence**, | and · be | no · more | seen.

Occasional Anthems. 39

96. T. MORLEY.

97. REV. J. FLINTOFT.

BURIAL OF THE DEAD.—(CONTINUED.)

LORD, **Thou** hast | been · our | refuge : ‖ from **one** gener- | a-tion | to · an- | other.

Before the mountains were brought forth, or ever the **earth** and the | world · were | made : ‖ Thou art God from **everlasting**, and | world · with- | out · = | end.

Thou turnest **man** | to · de- | struction : ‖ again Thou sayest, **Come** a- | gain, · ye | children · of | men.

For a thousand years in Thy **sight** are | but · as | yesterday : ‖ seeing that is **past** | as · a | watch · in the | night.

As soon as Thou scatterest them they are **even** | as · a | sleep : ‖ and fade **away** | sudden -ly | like · the | grass.

In the morning it is **green**, and | grow-eth | up : ‖ but in the evening it is cut **down**, | dri - ed | up, · and | withered.

For we consume **away** in | Thy · dis- | pleasure : ‖ and are **afraid** at Thy | wrath -ful | in - dig- | nation.

Thou hast set our **misdeeds** be- | fore · = | Thee : ‖ and our secret **sins** in the | light of · Thy | coun - te- | nance.

For when Thou art angry, **all** our | days · are | gone : ‖ we bring our years to an **end**, as it | were · a | tale that · is | told.

The days of our age are threescore years and ten ; and though men be so strong that they **come** to | four - score | years : ‖ yet is their strength then but labour and sorrow; so soon **passeth** it a- | way, · and | we · are | gone.

So teach **us** to | number · our | days : ‖ that we may apply our **hearts** | un-to | wis - = | dom.

Glory be to the **Father**, ¦ and · to the | Son : ‖ **and** | to · the | Ho-ly | Ghost;
As it was in the beginning, is **now**, and | ev - er | shall be : ‖ **world** with- | out · end. | A- = | men.

For Verse "I heard a voice," *See No.* 161.

Occasional Anthems.

98.

99.

100. W. H. WALTER. 1869.

101. J. JONES.

102. J. BARNBY.

Occasional Anthems. 41

103. P. FUSSELL.

Magnificat.
St. Luke I. 46.

My soul doth **magni-** | **fy** · the | Lord : ‖ and my spirit **hath** re- | joiced · in | God · my | Saviour.

For He | hath · re- | garded : ‖ the **lowliness** | of · His | hand- = | maiden.

For be- | hold, · from | henceforth : ‖ **all** gener- | ations · shall] call · me | blessed.

For He that is mighty hath **magni-** | fi - ed | me : ‖ **and** | ho - ly | is · His | Name.

And His mercy is on **them** that | fear · = | Him : ‖ **throughout** | all · = | gen - er - | ations.

He hath showed **strength** | with · His | arm : ‖ He hath scattered the **proud** in the imagin- | a - tion | of · their | hearts.

He hath put down the **mighty** | from · their | seat : ‖ and **hath** ex- | alted · the | humble · and | meek.

He hath filled the **hungry** | with · good | things : ‖ and the **rich** He | hath · sent | empty · a- | way.

He remembering His mercy hath holpen His **servant** | Is - ra- | el : ‖ as He promised to our forefathers, 'Abraham | and · his | seed, · for | ever.

Glory be to the **Father,** | and · to the | Son : ‖ **and** | to · the | Ho-ly | Ghost;

As it was in the beginning, is **now,** and | ev - er | shall be : ‖ **world** with- | out · end. | A - = | men.

Nunc dimittis.
St. Luke ii. 29.

Lord, now lettest Thou Thy **servant** de- | part · in | peace : ‖ **ac-** | cording | to · Thy | word.

For mine | eyes · have | seen : ‖ **Thy** | sal - = | va - = | tion,

Which **Thou** | hast · pre- | pared : ‖ **before** the | face · of | all · = | people;

To be a **light** to ! lighten · the | Gentiles : ‖ and to be the **glory** of Thy | peo - ple | Is - ra- | el.

Glory be to the **Father,** | and · to the | Son : ‖ **and** | to · the | Ho-ly | Ghost;

As it was in the beginning, is **now,** and | ev - er | shall be : ‖ **world** with- | out · end. | A - = | men.

The Gregorian Chant

Is composed of four parts: the *Intonation*, the *Dominant* (or *Reciting Note*), the *Mediation*, and the *Cadence*.

VIII. 1.

| Intonation | Dominant. | Mediation. | Dominant. | Cadence. |

Glo-ry ‖ be to the **Father**, and to the . . . | Sŏn : **and** . . . | tŏ the Hŏ-ly͡-Ghost;
As it ‖ was in the beginning, is **now**, and ever | shăll be: **world** with-| out end. A - men.

The *Intonation* should be used on all SUNDAYS and FESTIVALS at the beginning of the first verse of each Canticle, and also for every verse of the *Benedictus, Magnificat* and *Nunc Dimittis*. In this book the *Intonation* is used for every verse of the Anthems for EASTER DAY; for the Psalm at the CONSECRATION of a CHURCH, and INSTITUTION of MINISTERS, and also for each verse of the GLORIA PATRI.

In the above example, and in the pages following, the words placed before the short double bar (‖) belong to the *Intonation*, and should be sung rather slower than the rest. The words which follow the short double bar (‖) and precede the single bar (|) in either part of the Chant, belong to the *Dominant* (or Reciting Note). The last important word in the recitation is printed in heavier type, and when this word contains more than one syllable, the proper accent is indicated thus (^); as for instance, "**rejŏice**," "**prepâred**," "**generâtion**," &c.

In five of the Tones, (II., IV., V., VI., and VIII.) the *Mediation* is variable, having a final note which is used when the half-verse ends with an unaccented word or syllable, and omitted when the last word or syllable is accented. The dots (see example) separate the variable note from the other notes of the melody which are invariable. The accent marks in the text correspond with those placed over the notes of the *Mediation* and *Cadence*.

A syllable intended to be sung to two or more notes, is printed in *italics*.

When two words are to be sung to one note, they are joined by a short curve (͡), as in the second verse of the *Venite*.

The Tones are harmonized in "short score" for four voices, although it is generally conceded that the melody should be sung by all the voices in unisons and octaves, in which case the skillful organist may vary the accompaniment; taking care not to perplex the voices by an injudicious use of modern and chromatic harmonies.

To secure antiphonal effect the *odd* verses may be sung by Tenors and Basses in unison; the *even* verses by Treble voices; the *Gloria Patri* full, and in harmony.

Gregorian Tones. 43

Venite, exultemus Domino.

O || COME, let us **sing** unto the | Lòrd : let us heartily rejoice in the **strength** of | oùr · sal-và-tion.

Let us come before His presence with **thanks-** | gìv-ing : and **show** ourselves | glàd · in · Hìm · with⌢psalms.

For the **Lord** is a great | Gòd : and a great **King** a- | bòve · àll · gods.

In His hand are all the **corners** of the | èarth : and the strength of the **hills** is | *His* · àl-so.

The sea is **His**, and He | màde · it : and His **hands** pre- | pàr-ed · the⌢drỳ · land.

O come, let us **worship**, and fall | dòwn : and **kneel** before the | Lòrd · our · Mà-ker.

For He is the **Lord** our | Gòd : and we are the people of His **pasture**, and the | shèep · of · Hìs · hand.

O worship the Lord in the **beauty** of | hò-liness : let the whole **earth** | stànd · in · àwe · of⌢Him.

For He cometh, for He cometh to **judge** the | èarth : and with righteousness to judge the **world**, and the | pèo-ple · wìth · His⌢truth.

GLO-RY || be to the **Father**, and to the | Sòn : **and to** · the · Hò-ly⌢Ghost ;

As IT || was in the beginning, is **now**, and ever | shàll · be : **world** with- | òut · end. À-men.

Venite, exultemus Domino.

O || COME, let us **sing** | ùn-to · the⁀Lòrd : let us heartily rejoice in the **strength** of | òur · sal-và-tion.

Let us come before His **présence** with | *thànks*-gìv-ing : and **show** ourselves | glàd · in · Hìm · with · psalms.

For the **Lord** is a | *grèat* · Gòd : and a great **King** a- | *bòve · àll* · gods.

In His hand are all the **còrners** | ŏf · the · èarth : and the strength of the **hills** is | *H'is* · àl-so.

The sea is **His**, and | *Hè* · màde · it : and His **hands** pre- | pàr-ed · the⁀*dr'y* · land.

O come, let us **wòrship**, and | *fàll · dòwn* : and **knèel** before the | Lòrd · our · Mà - ker.

For **He** is the | Lòrd · our · Gòd : and we are the people of His **pàsture**, and the | shèep · of · *H'is* · hand.

O worship the **Lord** in the | bèauty · of · hò-liness : let the whole **earth** | stànd · in · àwe · of · Him.

For He cometh, for He **còmeth** to | jùdge · the · èarth : and with righteousness to judge the **world**, and the | pèo-ple · wìth · His · truth.

GLO-RY || be to the **Fàther**, | ànd · to · the⁀Sòn : **and** | tò · the · Hò-ly · Ghost;

As IT || was in the beginning, is **now**, and | èv-er · shàll · be : **world** with- | òut · end. À-men.

Gregorian Tones. 45

Venite, exultemus Domino.

O || come, let us **sing** | ùn-to · the ͡Lòrd : let us heartily **rejóice** in the | strèngth · of · oùr · sal-và-tion.

Let us come before His **présence** with | *thànks* - gìv - ing : and show ourselves **glad** in | *Hìm · wìth · psâlms.*

For the **Lord** is a | *grèat · Gòd* : and a great **King** a- | *bòve · àll · gòds.*

In His hand are all the **córners** | òf · the · èarth : and the strength of the **hills** | *is · Hìs · àl-so.*

The sea is **His**, and | *Hè · màde · it* : and His **hands** pre- | pàr-ed · the ͡drỳ · lànd.

O come, let us **wòrship**, and | *fàll · dòwn* : and **kneel** be- | fore · the · Lòrd · our · Mà - ker.

For **He** is the | Lòrd · our · Gòd : and we are the people of His **pàsture**, and the | shèep · of · Hìs · hànd.

O worship the **Lord** in the | bèauty · of | hò-liness : let the whole **earth** | stànd · in · àwe · of · Hìm.

For He cometh, for He **còmeth** to | jùdge · the · èarth : and with righteousness to judge the **world**, and the | pèo-ple · wìth · His · *truth.*

Glo-ry || be to the **Fàther**, | ànd · to · the ͡Sòn : **and** | tò · the · Hò-ly · *Ghòst;*

As it || was in the beginning, is **now**, and | èv-er · shàll · be : **world** with- | òut · end. À-*men.*

32

Gregorian Tones.

Te Deum laudamus.

Priest.	Full.
	We praise Thee, O God : we **acknowledge** | Thee · to · be · the⌢Lord.
Full.	All the **earth** doth | wŏr-ship · Thĕe : the **Fàther** | ĕv-er-làst-ing.
Dec.	To Thee all **Angels** ¦ crȳ · a-lŏud : the **Heavens**, and | àll · the · Pŏwers · therein.
Can.	To Thĕe **Chĕrubim** and | Sĕ-raph-ìm : **con-** | tìn-ual-lȳ · do⌢cry,
Full.	**Hòly,** | Hòly, · Hò-ly : **Lord** | Gòd · of · Sà-baoth ; Heaven and earth are **full** | ŏf · the · Mà-jesty : * | ŏf · Thy · glò-ry.
Dec.	The glorious **còmpany** | ŏf · the⌢A-pòs-tles : * | prǎise · = · ` = · Thee.
Can.	The goodly **fèllowship** | ŏf · the · Prò-phets : * | prǎise · = · ` = · Thee.
Dec.	The **nòble** | àr-my⌢of · Màr-tyrs : * | prǎise · = · ` = · Thee.
Can.	The holy **Church** throughout | àll · the · wòrld : **doth** | ` = · ac-knŏw-ledge⌢Thee ;
Dec.	**The** | Fà- = · ` = · ther : **of** an | ìn-finite · Mà-jesty ;
Can.	**Thine** a- ¦ dòr-able, · trŭe : **and** | ŏn- = · ` = · lȳ⌢Son ;
Dec.	**Alsŏ** the | Hŏ-ly · Ghŏst : **the** | Còm- = · ` = · forter.
Full.	**Thŏu** art the | Kìng · of · glò-ry : * | `O · = · ` = · Christ. Thou **art** the ever- | làst-ing · Sŏn : **of** | thĕ · = · Fà-ther.
Dec.	When Thou tookest upon **Thee** to de- | lìv-er · màn : Thou didst humble Thyself to be **born** | ŏf · a · Vìr-gin.
Can.	When Thou hadst **overcŏme** the ¦ shàrp-ness⌢of · dĕath : Thou didst open the kingdom of **Heaven** to | àll · be-lìev-ers.
Dec.	Thou sittest **at** the | right · hand⌢of . Gŏd : in the **glŏry** | ŏf · the · Fà-ther.
Can.	We **belìeve** that | Thŏu · shalt · cŏme : **to** | bĕ · = · ŏur · Judge.
Dec.	We therefore **pray** Thee, | hèlp · Thy · sèr-vants : whom Thou hast **redĕemed** | with · Thy · prè-cious⌢blood.
Can.	Make them to be **nŭmbered** | with · Thy · Sàints : in **glŏry** | ĕv-er-làst-ing.
Dec.	O **Lord,** | sàve · Thy · pĕo-ple : **and** | blèss · Thine · hèr-itage.
Can.	**Gŏv-** | ĕrn · thĕm : and **lift** them | ùp · for · ĕv-er.
Full.	**Day** | bȳ · dày : **we** | màg-ni-fȳ · Thĕe ; And we | wŏrship · Thy · Nàme : **ĕver** | wŏrld · with-òut · end.
Dec.	**Vouchsàfe,** | `O · Lòrd : to **keep** us | thìs · day⌢with-òut · sin.
Can.	O **Lord,** have | mèr-cy⌢up-ŏn · us : **have** | mèr-cy⌢up-ŏn · us.
Dec.	O Lord, let Thy **mèrcy** | bĕ · up-ŏn · us : **as** our | trùst · is · in · Thee.
Full.	O Lord, in **Thee** | hàve · I · trùst-ed : let me **nĕver** | bĕ · con-found-ed.

---

* Omit the reciting note.   F

Gregorian Tones.

Benedicite, omnia opera Domini.

O = ‖ ALL ye Works of the **Lord**, | bless · ye · the⁀*Lòrd* : praise **Him**, and | màgni-fy · Him · for · èv-er.

   O ye Angels of the **Lord**, | bless · ye · the⁀*Lòrd* : praise **Him**, and | màgni-fy · Him · for · èv-er.

   O ye **Heavens**, | bless · ye · the⁀*Lòrd* : praise **Him**, and | màgni-fy · Him · for · èv-er.

   O ye Waters that be above the **Firmament**, | bless · ye · the⁀*Lòrd* : praise **Him**, and | màgni-fy · Him · for · èv-er.

   O all ye Powers of the **Lord**, | bless · ye · the⁀*Lòrd* : praise **Him**, and | màgni-fy · Him · for · èv-er.

   O ye Sun and **Moon**, | bless · ye · the⁀*Lòrd* : praise **Him**, and | màg-ni-fy · Him · for · èv-er.

   O ye Stars of **Heaven**, | bless · ye · the⁀*Lòrd* : praise **Him**, and | màgni-fy · Him · for · èv-er.

   O ye Showers and **Dew**, | bless · ye · the⁀*Lòrd* : praise **Him**, and | màgni-fy · Him · for · èv-er.

   O ye Winds of **God**, | bless · ye · the⁀*Lòrd* : praise **Him**, and | màgni-fy · Him · for · èv-er.

---

* For Tone III. 4, disregard the accent on the word "magnify," and the bar before it.

† For Tone V. 1, omit the accents on the words "bless" and "magnify," and the bars next before.

Gregorian Tones.

O ye Fire and **Heat,** | blèss · ye · the⁀*Lòrd*: praise **Him,** and | màg-ni-fy · Hìm · for · èv-er.

O ye Winter and **Summer,** | blèss · ye · the⁀*Lòrd* : praise **Him,** and | màgni-fy : Hìm · for · èv-er.

O ye Dews and **Frosts,** | blèss · ye · the⁀*Lòrd* : praise **Him,** and | màgni-fy · Hìm · for · èv-er.

O ye Frost and **Cold,** | blèss · ye the⁀*Lòrd* : praise **Him,** and | màg-ni-fy · Hìm · for · èv-er.

O ye Ice and **Snow,** | blèss · ye · the⁀*Lòrd* : praise **Him,** and | màg-ni-fy · Hìm · for · èv-er.

O ye Nights and **Days,** | bless · ye · the⁀*Lòrd* : praise **Him,** and | màgni-fy · Him · for · èv-er.

O ye Light and **Darkness,** | blèss · ye · the⁀*Lòrd* : praise **Him,** and | màgni-fy · Hìm · for · èv-er.

O ye Lightnings and **Clouds,** | blèss · ye · the⁀*Lòrd* : praise **Him,** and | màgni-fy · Hìm · for · èv-er.

O let the **Earth,** | blèss · — the⁀*Lòrd* : **Yea,** let it praise **Him,** and | màgni-fy · Hìm · for · èv-er.

O ye Mountains and **Hills,** | blèss · ye · the⁀*Lòrd* : praise **Him,** and | màgni-fy · Hìm · for · èv-er.

O all ye Green Things upon the **Earth,** | blèss · ye · the⁀*Lòrd* : praise **Him,** and | màgni-fy · Hìm · for · èv-er.

O ye **Wells,** | blèss · ye · the⁀*Lòrd* : praise **Him,** and | màgni-fy · Hìm · for · èv-er.

O ye Seas and **Floods,** | blèss · ye · the⁀*Lòrd* : praise **Him,** and | màgni-fy · Hìm · for · èv-er.

O ye **Whales,** and all that move in the **waters,** | blèss · ye · the⁀*Lòrd* : praise **Him,** and | màgni-fy · Hìm · for · èv-er.

O all ye Fowls of the **Air,** | blèss · ye · the⁀*Lòrd* : praise **Him,** and | màgni-fy · Hìm · for · èv-er.

O all ye Beasts and **Cattle,** | blèss · ye · the⁀*Lòrd* : praise **Him,** and | màgni-fy · Hìm · for · èv-er.

O ye children of **Men,** | blèss · ye · the⁀*Lòrd* : praise **Him,** and | màg-ni-fy · Hìm · for · èv-er.

O let **Israel** | blèss · — the⁀*Lòrd* : praise **Him,** and | màgni-fy · Hìm · for · èv-er.

O ye Priests of the **Lord,** | blèss · ye · the⁀*Lòrd* : praise **Him,** and | màgni-fy · Hìm · for · èv-er.

O ye Servants of the **Lord,** | blèss · ye · the⁀*Lòrd* : praise **Him,** and | màgni-fy · Hìm · for · èv-er.

O ye Spirits and Souls of the **Righteous,** | blèss · ye · the⁀*Lòrd* : praise **Him,** and | màgni-fy · Hìm · for · èv-er.

O ye holy and humble Men of **Heart,** | blèss · ye · the⁀*Lòrd* : praise **Him,** and | màgni-fy · Him · for · èv-er.

GLO-RY ‖ be to the **Father,** | ànd · to · the⁀*Son* : **and** | tò · the · Hŏ-ly · Ghŏst. As IT ‖ was in the beginning, is **now,** and | èv-er · shall · be : **world** with-| òut · end. · *A - men.*

Jubilate Deo.

Psalm c.

O · BE ‖ joyful in the **Lord** | àll · ye · lànds : serve the Lord with gladness, and come **befôre** His | prè - sence · with · a · song.

Be ye sure that the **Lord,** | Hè · is · God : it is He that hath made us, and not we ourselves ; we are His people, and the **sheep** | òf · His · *pàs* - ture.

O go your way into His gates with thanksgiving, and **into** His | còurts · with · pràise : be thankful unto **Him,** and | speak · good · òf · His · Name.

For the Lord is gracious, His **mèrcy** is | èv - er - làst - ing : and His truth endureth from **generàtion** to | gèn - er - à - tion.

GLO-RY ‖ be to the **Fàther,** | ànd · to · the Sòn : **and** | tò · the · Hò-ly · Ghost;

As · IT ‖ was in the beginning, is **now,** and | èv - er · shàll · be : **world** with- | òut · end. | A-men.

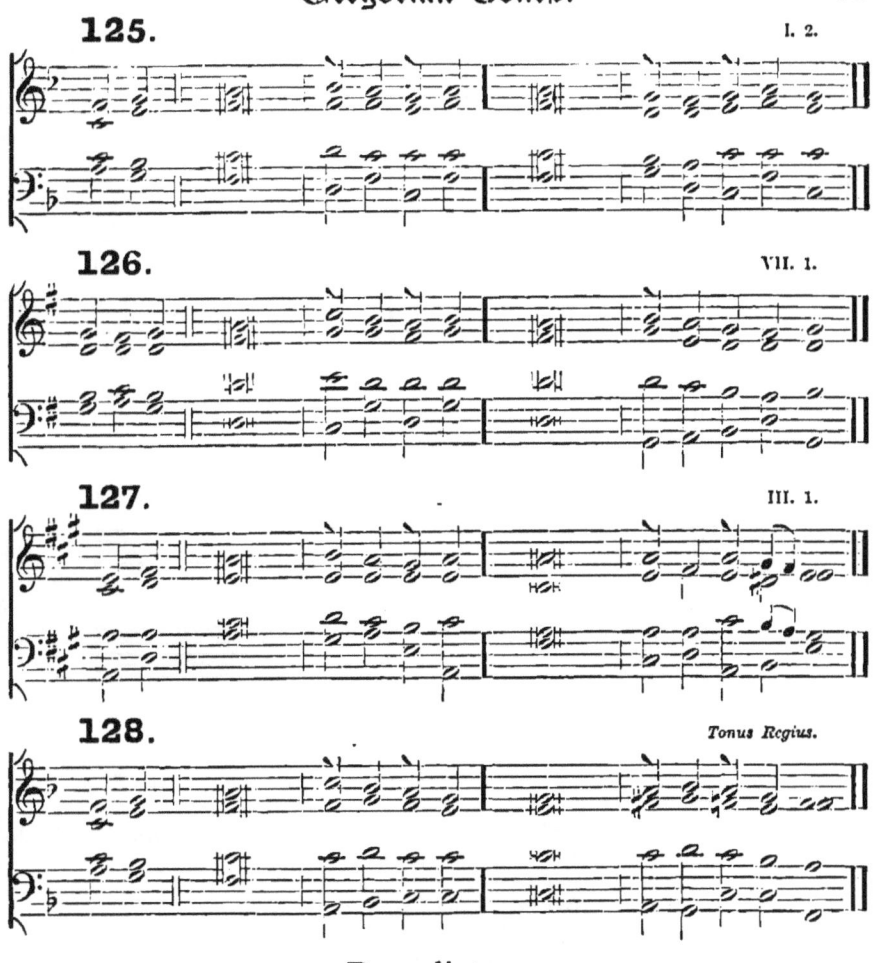

Benedictus.

St. Luke i. 68.

BLESS-ED ‖ be the Lord **God** of | Is-ra-*ël* : for He hath visited and **redeemed** | *His* · *pèo*-ple ;

And hath ‖ raised up a mighty **salvation** | *fòr* · *ùs* : in the **house** of His | *sèr*-vant · *Dà*-vid ;

As He ‖ spake by the **mouth** of His | hò - ly · Prò - phets : which have **been** | since · the | wòrld · be - gan ;

That = ‖ we should be **saved** | fròm · our | èn - emies : and from the **hand** of | àll · that · *hàte* · us.

GLO - RY ‖ be to the **Father** | ànd · to the · *Sòn* : **and** | tò · the · Hò-ly · Ghost;

As · IT ‖ was in the beginning, is **now**, and | èv - er · shàll · be : **world** with - | òut · end. | *A* - men.

Gregorian Tones.

Cantate Domino.
Psalm xcviii.

O ‖ sing unto the **Lord** a | *nèw · sòng* : for **He** | hàth · done · màr-vellous · things.

With His own right **hand**, and with His | hò-ly · *àrm* : hath He **gôtten** Him- | sèlf · the · vìc-to-ry.

The Lord **declàred** | His · sal-va-tion : His righteousness hath He openly **shôwed** in the | sìght · of⌒the | *hèa*-then.

He hath remembered His mercy and truth **towàrd** the | hòuse of · Is-rael : and all the ends of the world have **seen** the sal- | vù-tion · òf · our · God.

Show yourselves joyful unto the **Lord,** | àll · ye *lànds* : **sing,** re- | joìce, and · *gìve* · thanks.

Praise the **Lord** up- | òn · the · *hàrp* : sing to the harp with a **psalm** of | *thànks - gìv* - ing.

With **trûmpets** | àl-so · and⌒*shawms* : O show yourselves **jôyful** be- | fòre · the · Lòrd, · the · King.

Let the sea make a noise, and **all** that | thère-in · *ìs* : the round **world,** and | thèy · that · dwèll · there-in.

Let the floods clap their hands, and let the hills be joyful **togèther** be- | fòre · the · *Lòrd* : for **He** | còm - eth⌒to · jùdge · the · earth.

With righteousness **shall** He | jùdge · the · *wòrld* : **and** the | pèo - ple⌒with · è - qui - ty.

Glo-ry ‖ be to the **Fàther,** | ànd · to · the⌒Sòn : **and** | tò · the · Hò-ly · Ghost;

As · it ‖ was in the beginning, is **now,** and | èv - er · shàll · be: **world** with - | òut · end. | *A* - men.

Bonum est confiteri.
Psalm xcii.

It · is ‖ a good thing to give **thanks** unto the | Lòrd : and to sing praises unto Thy **Name,** | ʽO · Most · Hìgh - est.

To tell of Thy loving-kindness **èarly** in the | mòrn-ing : and of Thy **truth** in the | *nìght* · sèa - son.

Upon an instrument of ten **strings,** and upon the | lùte : upon a loud **instrument,** | ànd · up - òn · the⁀harp.

For Thou, Lord, hast made me **glad** through Thy | wòrks : and I will rejoice in giving **praise** for the oper- | à - tions · of⁀Thỳ · hands.

Glo-ry ‖ be to the **Fàther,** and to the | Sòn : **and** | tò · the · Hò-ly⁀Ghost ;

As · it ‖ was in the beginning, is **now,** and ever | shàll · be : **world** with- | òut · end.   ʽA - men.

Gregorian Tones.

136.   I. 1.

137.   I. 6.

138.   V. 5. (*Rouen Mediation.*)

Deus misereatur.
Psalm lxvii.

GOD · BE ‖ **mèrciful** unto | ùs, · and · blèss · us : and show us the light of His countenance, **and** be | mèrci - ful · ùn - to · *ùs* ;

    That Thy **way** may be | knòwn · upon · *èarth* : Thy saving **health** a- | mòng · àll · nà - tions.

    Let the people **praise** | Thèe, · O · *Gòd* : yea, let **all** the | pèo-ple · *pràise · Thèe.*

    O let the nations **rejôice**, | ànd · be · *glàd* : for Thou shalt judge the folk righteously, and **gòvern** the | nà - tions⌢up - òn · *èarth*.

    Let the people **praise** | Thèe, · O · *Gòd* : yea, let **all** the | pèo-ple · *pràise · Thèe.*

    Then shall the **earth** bring | fòrth · her · *in-crease* : and God, even our own **God**, shall | gìve · us · *Hìs* · bless-ìng.

    God shall | *blèss · ùs* : and all the **ends** of the | wòrld · shall · *fèar · Hìm*.

GLO - RY ‖ be to the **Fàther** | ànd · to · the⌢*Sòn* : **and** | tò · the · Hò-ly · *Ghòst;*

As · IT ‖ was in the beginning, is **now**, and | èv - er · shàll · be : **world** with - | òut · end. *À - mèn.*

Gregorian Tones. 55

Deus misereatur.
Psalm lxvii.

GOD · BE ‖ **merciful** unto | ùs, · and · blèss · us : and show us the light of His countenance, **and** be | mèrci - ful · ùn - to · ùs ;-

That Thy **way** may be | knòwn · upon · *earth* : Thy saving **health** a- | mòng · all · *nà* - tiòns.

Let the people **praise** | Thèe, · O · *Gòd* : yea, let **all** the | pèo-ple · *pràise* · Thèe.

O let the nations **rejóice**, | ànd · be · *glàd* : for Thou shalt judge the folk righteously, and **góvern** the | nù - tions ͡ up - òn · èarth.

Let the people **praise** | Thèe, · O · *Gòd* : yea, let **all** the | pèo-ple · *pràise* · Thèe.

Then shall the **earth** bring | fòrth · her · ìn-crease : and God, even our own God, shall **give** | ùs · His · *blèss* - ing.

God shall | *blèss* · *ùs* : and all the **ends** of the | wòrld · shall · *fèar* · Hìm.

GLO - RY ‖ be to the **Fáther** | ànd · to · the ͡ *Sòn* : **and** | tò · the · Hò-ly · Ghòst;

As · IT ‖ was in the beginning, is **now**, and | èv - er · shàll · be : **world** with - | òut · end. *A* - mèn.

---

* This note should be used for the last syllable in the recitation.

Gregorian Tones.

Benedic, anima mea.*
Psalm ciii.

PRAISE = ‖ the **Lord,** | `O · my · *soùl* : and all that is **within** me | pràise · His · hò - ly · Name.

Praise the **Lord,** `O · my · *soùl* : and forget **not** | àll · His · bè - ne - fits ;

Who **forgiveth** | àll · thy · *sìn* : and healeth **all** | thìne · in - fìrm - i - ties ;

Who saveth thy **life** | fròm · de - | strùction : and crowneth thee with **mèrcy** and | lòv - ing - *kìnd* - ness ;

O praise the Lord, ye Angels of His, ye that ex- | cèl · in · *strèngth* : ye that fulfil His commandment, and **hèarken** unto the | vòice · of · *His* · word.

O praise the **Lord,** all | yè · His · *hòsts* : ye servants of **His** that | dò · His · *plèa* - sure.

O speak good of the Lord, all ye works of His, in all **plàces** of | His · do- | mìn - ion : praise thou the **Lord,** | `O · *mỳ* · soul.

GLO - RY ‖ be to the **Fàther** | ànd · to ͡ the · *Sòn* : **and** | tò · the · Hò-ly · Ghost;
AS · IT ‖ was in the beginning, is **now,** and | òv - er · shàll · be : **world** with - | òut · end. | *À* - men.

<small>* This pointing may be used for VIII. 1, VIII. 2, V. 1, and V. 2, by omitting the first accent in the mediation.</small>

Gregorian Tones.

145. VIII. 1.

146. VIII. 2.

147. V. 3.

Easter Day.

Instead of "O come, let us sing," &c.

Christ our ‖ Passover is **sacrificed** | for · us : **therefore** | let · us · keep · the⌢feast;

Not with ‖ the old leaven, neither with the leaven of **malice** and | wickedness : but with the unleavened **bread** of sin- | cer · i · ty · and⌢truth. 1 *Cor.* v. 7.

Christ be- ‖ ing raised from the **dead**, dieth no | more : death hath no **more** do- | min-ion · o-ver⌢Him.

For in ‖ that He died, He died unto **sin** | once : but in that He **liveth**, He | liv-eth · un-to⌢God.

Like - wise ‖ reckon ye also yourselves to be dead **indeed** unto | sin : but alive unto **God** through | Je-sus · Christ · our⌢Lord. *Rom.* vi. 9.

Christ is ‖ **risen** from the | **dead** : and become the **first-** | fruits · of · them · that⌢slept.

For since ‖ by **man** came | **death** : by man came **also** the resur- | rec-tion · of · the⌢dead.

For as ‖ in **Adam** all | die : even so in **Christ** shall | all · be · made · alive. 1 *Cor.* xv. 20.

Glo - ry ‖ be to the **Father**, and to the | **Son** : **and** | to · the · Ho-ly⌢Ghost;

As · it ‖ was in the beginning, is **now**, and ever | shall · be : **world** with- | out · end. A-men.

Thanksgiving Day.

Instead of "O come, let us sing," &c.

PRAISE ye ‖ the Lord, for it is good to sing **praises** unto our | **God** : for it is **pleasant**, and | **praise** · is · **come**-ly.

  The Lord doth **build up** Je- | ru-salem : He gathereth **together** the | out-casts⁀of · Is-rael.

  He healeth those that are **broken** in | heart : **and** | bind-eth · up · their⁀wounds.

  He covereth the heaven with clouds, and prepareth **rain** for the | earth : He maketh the grass to **grow** up- | on · the · moun-tains.

  He giveth to the **beast** his | food : **and** to the | young · ravens · which⁀cry.

PRAISE = ‖ the **Lord**, O Je- | ru-salem : praise thy **God**, | ˋO · Si - on.

  For He hath strengthened the **bars** of thy | gates : He hath **blessed** thy | child-ren · with-in · thee.

  He maketh **peace** in thy | bor-ders ; and filleth **thee** with the | fi-nest · of the⁀wheat.

GLO - RY ‖ be to the **Father**, and to the | Son : **and** | to · the · Ho-ly⁀Ghost;

As · IT ‖ was in the beginning, is **now**, and ever | shall · be : **world** with- | out · end. A-men

Consecration of Churches.

Domini est terra.*
Psalm xxiv.

The earth||	is the Lord's, and all that therein | is : the compass of the world, and | they · that · dwell · therein.
For He ||	hath founded it upon the | seas : and prepared | it · up-on · the ͡floods.
Who shall ||	ascend into the hill of the | Lord : or who shall rise up | in · His · ho-ly ͡place?
Ev - en ||	he that hath clean hands, and a pure | heart : and that hath not lift up his mind unto vanity, nor sworn to de- | ceive · his · neigh-bour.
He shall ||	receive the blessing from the | Lord : and righteousness from the God of | his · sal-va-tion.
This is ||	the generation of them that | seek · Him : even of them that seek thy | face, · O · Ja-cob.
Lift up ||	your heads, O ye gates, and be ye lift up, ye ever- | last-ing ͡doors : and the King of | glo-ry · shall · come ͡in.
Who is ||	the King of | glo-ry : it is the Lord strong and mighty, even the Lord | mighty · in · bat-tle.
Lift up ||	your heads, O ye gates, and be ye lift up, ye ever- | last-ing ͡doors: and the King of | glo-ry · shall · come ͡in.
Who is ||	the King of | glo-ry : Even the Lord of hosts, He is the | King · of · glo-ry.
Glo - ry ||	be to the Father, and to the | Son : and | to · the · Ho-ly ͡Ghost ;
As it ||	was in the beginning, is now, and ever | shall · be : world with- | out · end. 'A-men.

Institution of Ministers.

Laudate Nomen.*

O praise ||	the Lord, laud ye the Name of the | Lord : praise it, O ye | ser-vants · of · the ͡Lord.
Ye that ||	stand in the house of the | Lord : in the courts of the | house · of · our · God.
O praise ||	the Lord, for the Lord is | gra-cious : O sing praises unto His Name, for | it · is · love-ly.
The Lord ||	is gracious and | mer-ciful : long-suffering, and of | great · good-ness.
The Lord ||	is loving unto eve-ry ͡man : and His mercy is | o-ver · all · His ͡works.
All Thy ||	works praise Thee, O | Lord : and Thy saints give | thanks · un-to ͡Thee.
The Lord ||	doth build up Je- | ru-salem : and gather together the | out-casts ͡of · 'Is-rael.
He heal- ||	eth those that are broken in | heart : and giveth medicine to | heal · their · sick-ness.
The Lord's ||	delight is in them that | fear · Him : and put their trust | in · His · mer-cy.
Praise = ||	the Lord, O Je- | ru-salem : praise thy God, | 'O · Si-on.
For He ||	hath made fast the bars of thy | gates : and hath blessed thy | child-ren · within · thee.
He mak- ||	eth peace in thy | bor-ders : and filleth thee | with · the · flour · of ͡wheat.
He is ||	our God, even the God of whom cometh sal- | va-tion : God is the Lord by | whom · we ͡es-cape · death.
O = ||	God, wonderful art Thou in Thy holy | pla-ces : even the God of Israel, He will give strength and power unto His people. | Bless-ed · be · God.
Glo - ry ||	be to the Father, and to the | Son : and | to · the · Ho-ly ͡Ghost ;
As it ||	was in the beginning, is now, and ever | shall · be : world with- | out · end. 'A-men.

---

* To be sung to either of the Tones on page 58.

Occasional Anthems.

151. I. 1.

152. V. 5. [Rouen Mediation.]

153. III. 4.

Magnificat.
St. Luke i. 46.

My = ‖ soul doth **magni-** | fy · the · Lòrd : and my spirit hath **rejòiced** in | Gòd · my · Sà-viour.

For = ‖ **He** | hàth · re-gàrd-ed : the **lôwliness** of | *H'is* · hànd-màid-en.

For be- ‖ **hòld** from | *hènce-fòrth* : all **generàtions** shall | càll · mè · Blèss-ed.

For = ‖ He that is **mighty** hath | mȧg-ni-fi-ed⁀me : **and** | hò-ly · is · His · Nàme.

And His ‖ **mèrcy** is on | thèm · that · fèar · Him : **throughôut** | àll · gèner-à-tions.

He hath ‖ shewed **strength** | with · His · àrm : He hath scattered the **proud** in the imagin- | à-tion · òf · their · *hèarts*.

He hath ‖ put down the **mighty** | from · their · *sèat* : and hath **exàlted** the | hùm-ble · ànd · mèek.

He hath ‖ filled the **hûngry** | with · good · *things* : and the rich He hath **sent** | èmp-ty · a-wày.

He · re- ‖ membering His mercy hath **hôlpen** His | sèr-vant · 'Is-rael : as He promised to our forefathers, **Abraham** and his | *sèed · fòr · èv-er.*

Glo-ry ‖ be to the **Fàther** | ànd · to · the⁀Sòn : **and** | tò · the · Hò-ly · *Ghòst ;*

As · it ‖ was in the beginning, is **now**, and | èv-er · shàll · be : **world** with- | òut · ènd. 'A - men.

Occasional Anthems. 61

Nunc dimittis.
St. Luke ii. 29.

Lord, = ‖ now lettest Thou Thy **servant** de- | pàrt · in · *pèace* : **ac-** | còr-ding · tò · Thy · word.

For = ‖ **mine** | èyes · have · *sèen* : **Thy** | `= · sal -rà- tion.

Which =‖ **Thou** | hàst · pre - pàr - ed : before the **face** of | *àll · pèo* - ple ;

To be ‖ a **light** to | light - en · the⌒Gèn-tiles : and to be the **glóry** of Thy | pèo - ple · `Is - ra - el.

Glo - ry ‖ be to the **Father**, | ànd · to · the⌒*Sòn* : **and** | tò · the · Hò-ly · Ghost;

As · it ‖ was in the beginning, is **now**, and | èv - er · shàll · be : **world** with - | òut · end. *À* - mèn.

158. Burial of the Dead.

W. H. WALTER.

¶ *The Minister .... shall say, or sing:*

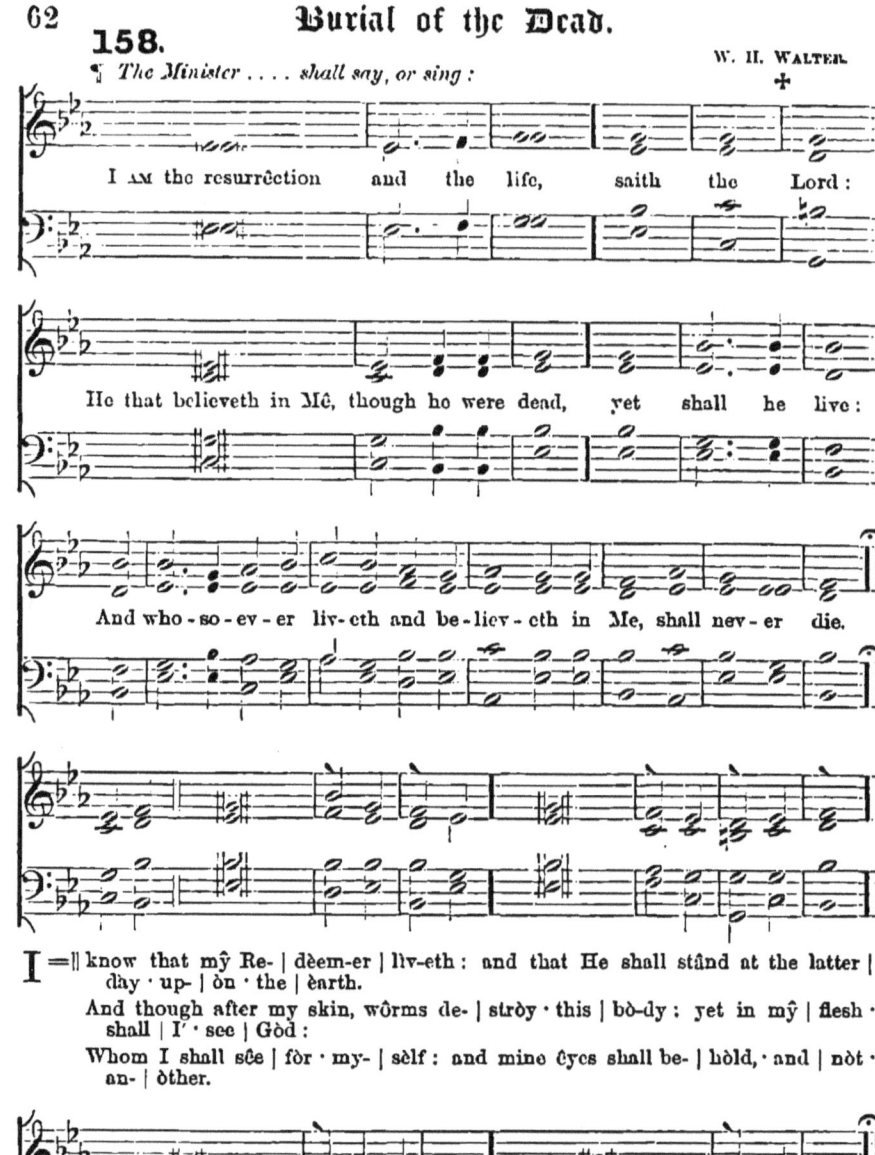

I know that mŷ Re- | dèem-er | lĭv-eth: and that He shall stând at the latter | dày · up- | òn · the | èarth.

And though after my skin, wŏrms de- | strŏy · this | bŏ-dy: yet in mŷ | flesh · shall | I' · see | Gŏd:

Whom I shall sĕe | fòr · my- | sèlf: and mine ĕyes shall be- | hòld, · and | nòt an- | òther.

We brought nŏthing | ĭn-to · this | world: and it is cĕrtain we can carry | nŏ-thing | out.

The Lord gave, and the Lôrd hath | tak-en · a- | way: blessed be the Nâme | of · the | Lord.

Burial of the Dead. 63

159.

¶ *After they are come into the Church, shall be said or sung the following Anthem.*

Lord, =‖ let me know my end, and the number | òf · my · dàys : that I may be certified how lông I | hàve · to · *live*.
Behold, Thou hast made my dàys as it | wère · a · spàn · long : and mine age is even as nothing in respect of Thee ; and verily every man living is àlto- | gèth-er · vàn-ity.
For man walketh in a vain shadow, and disquieteth him- | sèlf · in · vàin : he heapeth up riches, and cannot tell | whò · shall · gàth - er‿them.
And now, Lôrd | whàt‿is · my hôpe : Truly my hôpe is | èven · in · *Thèe*.
Deliver me from àll | mine ⁒ of-fèn-ces : and make me not a rebûke | unto · the · fòol-ish.
When Thou with rebukes dost chasten man for sin, Thou makest his beauty to consume away, like as it were a môth | frètting · a · gàr-ment : every man thèrefore | is · but · vàn-ity.
Hear my prayer, O Lord, and with Thine ears, con- | sìder · my · càll-ing : hold not Thy pêace | àt my *tèars ;*
For I àm a | strànger · with · Thèe ; and a sôjourner, as | àll · my · fà-thers‿were.
O spare me a little, that I mày re- | còver · my · strèngth : before I go hènce, and be | nô · more · *sèen*.

Lord, =‖ Thou hast been our | rè-fuge : from one generâtion to an- | ò-ther.
Before the mountains were brought forth, or ever the earth and the wôrld were ǀ made : Thou art God from everlasting, and wôrld with- | òut · end.
Thou turnest mân to de- | strùc-tion : again Thou sayest, Come agâin, ye chil-dren | òf · men.
For a thousand years in Thy sight are bùt as | yès-terday : seeing that is past as a wàtch | in · the‿night.
As soon as Thou scatterest them they are even às a | slèep : and fade away sùddenly ǀ like · the‿grass.
In the morning it is grêen, and groweth | ùp : but in the evening it is cut down, dried ûp, and | wìth-ered.
For we consume away in Thŷ dis- | plèa-sure : and are afraid at Thy wrùthful indig- | nà-tion.
Thou hast set our misdêeds be- | fôre · Thèe : and our secret sins in the light of Thy | còun-tenance.
For when Thou art angry, all our dâys are | gòne : we bring our years to an end, as it were a tâle that | ìs · told.
The days of our age are threescore years and ten ; and though men be so strong that they come to fôurscore | yèars : yet is their strength then but labour and sorrow ; so soon passeth it awây, and | wè · are‿gone.
So teach us to nûmber our | dàys : that we may apply our hèarts unto ǀ wìs-dom.
Glory be to the Fâther, and to the | Sòn : and tô the ǀ Hò-ly‿Ghost.
As it was in the beginning, is nôw, and ever | shàll · be : world without ènd. | A-men.

G

Burial of the Dead.

160.

¶ *When they come to the Grave, ... shall be sung or said:*

MAN, that ‖ is born of a woman, hath but a shórt | tíme · to | líve : and is fúll of | mis-ery.
He | còm-eth | ùp : and is cut dówn like a | flów-er.
He fléeth as it | wère · a | shàdow : and never contínueth in | òne · stay.
In the | mìdst · of | lìfe : we | àre · in ⁻death.
Of whom may we seek for súccour, but of | Thèe, O | Lòrd ; Who for our sins art jústly dis- | pléas-ed ?

Yet, O Lord, God most ho-ly : O Lord most might-y,

O holy and mòst merci-ful Saviour : { deliver us not into the bitter páins of e-ter-nal death;
Thou knowest, Lord, the sécrets } of our hearts : { shut not Thy merciful éars to our prayer ;

But spáre us, Lord most ho-ly : O God most Might-y,
O holy and merci-ful Saviour : Thou most wórthy Judge e - ter - nal,

Suffer us nót, at our last hour : for any páins of déath, to fall from Thee.

Burial of the Dead.

From henceforth bless- ed are the dead which die in the Lord; even so saith the Spir--it; for they rest from their la - - bours.

163.

De profundis.

Psalm cxxx.

Out of the deep have I called unto Thĕe, O | Lòrd : || Lôrd, hear my | vòice.
O let Thine ears consider | wèll : || the voice of mỹ com- | plàint.
If Thou, Lord, wilt be extreme to mark what is dône a- | mĭss : || O Lord, who mǎy a- | bĭde it.
For there is mèrcy with | Thĕe : || therefore shalt Thôu be | fĕared.
I look for the Lord, my soul doth wâit for | Hĭm : || in His wôrd is my | trŭst.
My soul fléeth unto the | Lòrd : || before the morning watch, I say before the mòrning | wàtch.
O Israel, trust in the Lord, for with the Lôrd there is | mèrcy : || and with Him is plènteous re- | dèmption.
And He shall redêem Isra- | ĕl : || from âll his | sĭns.

Glory be to the Father, and tô the | Sòn : || and to the Hôly | Ghòst ;
As it was in the beginning, is now, and êver shall | bĕ : || world without ênd. A- | mĕn.

Choral Service.

164.

For the SENTENCES, *the* EXHORTATION, CONFESSION, *and the* ABSOLUTION, *any convenient note may be taken.*

Minister and People. — Our Father, &c. — A-men.

Minister. — O Lord, o-pen Thou our lips.

Or this:

Answer. — And our mouth shall show forth Thy praise.

Minister. — Glory be to the Father, and to the Son, and to the Holy Ghost;

Answer. — As it was in the beginning, is now; and ev-er shall be, world without end. A-men.

Minister. — Praise ye the Lord.

Answer. — The Lord's Name be prais-ed.

Here follow the VENITE EXULTEMUS, *the* PSALMS, LESSONS, *and* CANTICLES, *in their appointed order.*

THE APOSTLES' CREED.

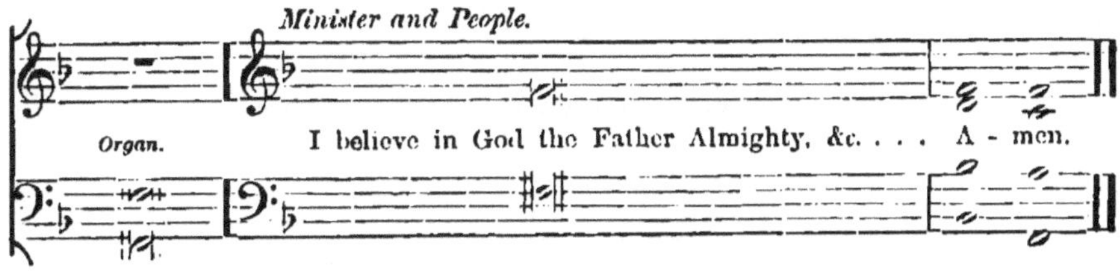

Minister and People.

Organ. — I believe in God the Father Almighty, &c. . . . . A-men.

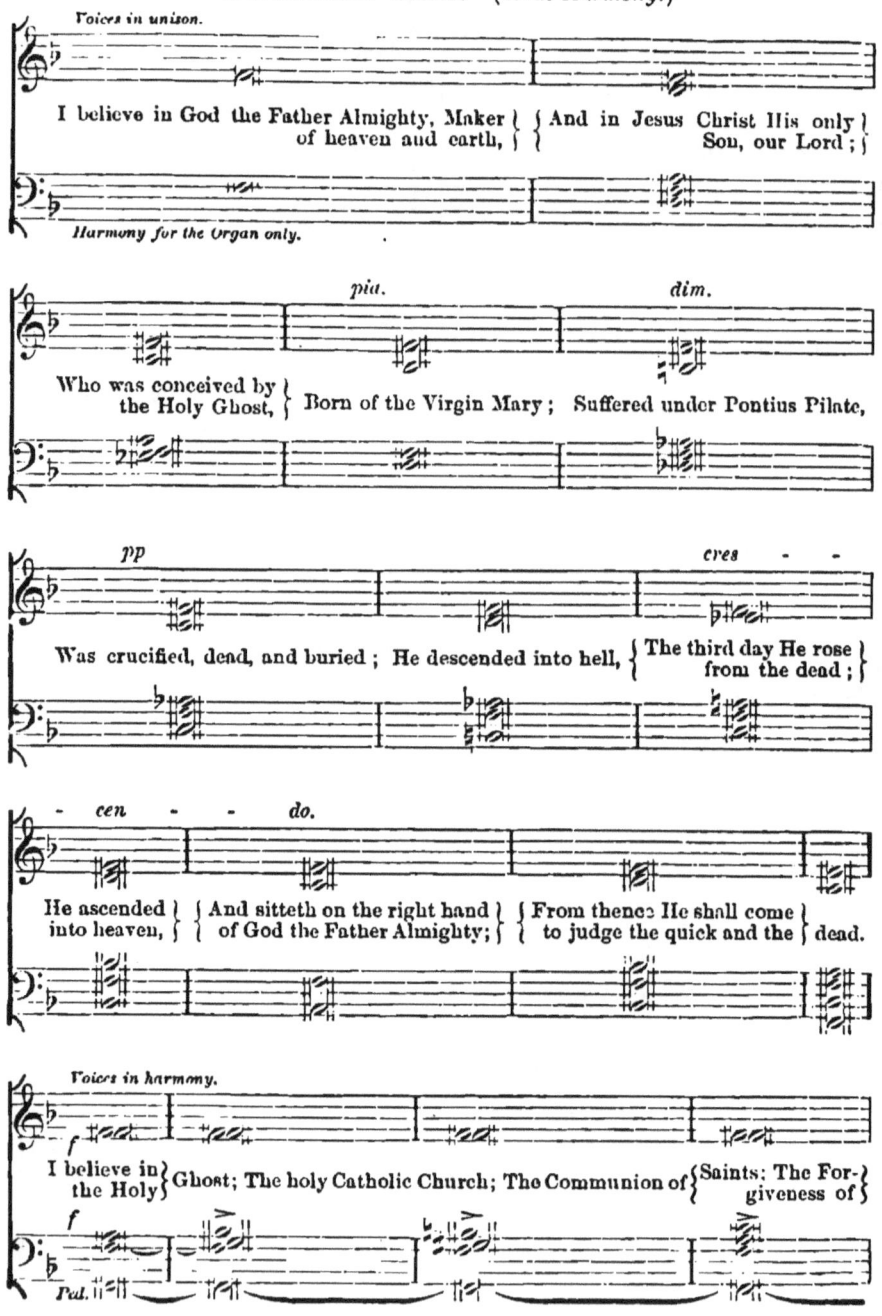

The Litany.

165.

Minister.

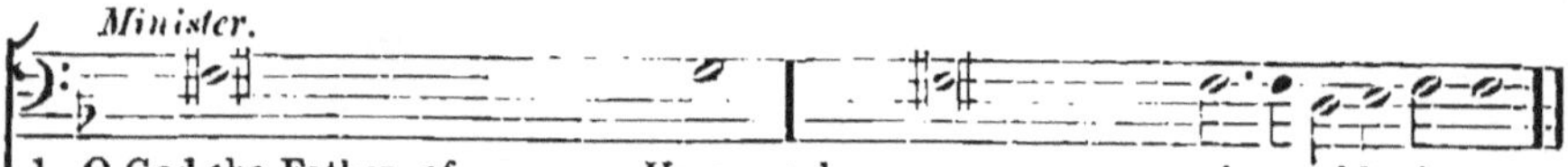

1. O God the Father, of Heaven : have mercy upon us mis-er-a-ble sinners.
2. O God the Son, Redeemer of the world : have mercy upon us mis-er-a-ble sinners,
3. O God the Holy Ghost, proceed- ing from the Father and the Son : have mercy upon us mis-er-a-ble sinners.
4. O holy, blessed, and glorious Trinity, three Persons and one God : have mercy upon us mis-er-a-ble sinners.

Choir.

1. O God the Father, of Heaven : have mercy upon us mis-er-a-ble sinners.
2. O God the Son, Redeemer of the world : have mercy upon us mis-er-a-ble sinners.
3. O God the Holy Ghost, proceeding from the Father and the Son : have mercy upon us mis-er-a-ble sinners.
4. O holy, blessed, and glorious Trinity, three Persons and one God : have mercy upon us mis-er-a-ble sinners.

Minister.   *Answer.*

Remember not, Lord, our offences, nor the offences of our forefathers ; neither take Thou vengeance of our sins : spare us, good Lord, spare Thy people, whom Thou hast redeemed with Thy most precious blood, and be not angry with............ | us for ever.   Spare us, good Lord.

Minister.   *Answer.*

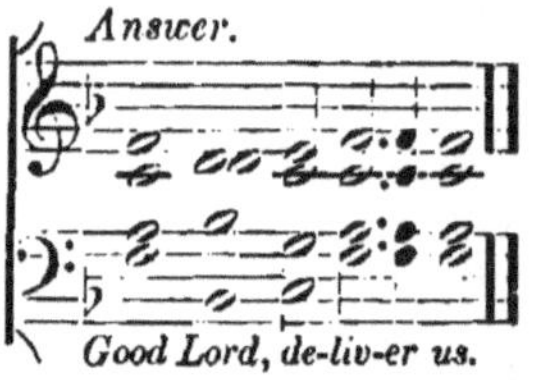

From all evil and mischief ; from sin ; from the crafts and assaults of the devil ; from Thy wrath, and from everlast- - - - - - - | ing dam-nation,   Good Lord, de-liv-er us.

From all blindness of heart ; from pride, vain-glory, and hypocrisy ; from envy, hatred, and malice, and all unchari- | ta-ble-ness,   *Good Lord, deliver us.*

From all inordinate and sinful affections ; and from all the deceits of the world, the flesh, | and the devil,   *Good Lord, deliver us.*

From lightning and tempest ; from plague, pestilence, and famine ; from battle and murder, and from | sud-den death,   *Good Lord, deliver us.*

From all sedition, privy conspiracy, and rebellion ; from all false doctrine, heresy, and schism ; from hardness of heart, and contempt of Thy Word | and Commandment,   *Good Lord, deliver us.*

By the mystery of Thy holy Incarnation ; by Thy holy Nativity and Circumcision ; by Thy Baptism, Fasting, | and Temp-tation,   *Good Lord, deliver us.*

By Thine Agony and Bloody Sweat ; by Thy Cross and Passion ; by Thy precious Death and Burial ; by Thy glorious Resurrection and Ascension ; and by the coming of the | Ho-ly Ghost,   *Good Lord, deliver us.*

In all time of our tribulation ; in all time of our prosperity ; in the hour of death, and in the | day of judgment,   *Good Lord, deliver us.*

The Litany.

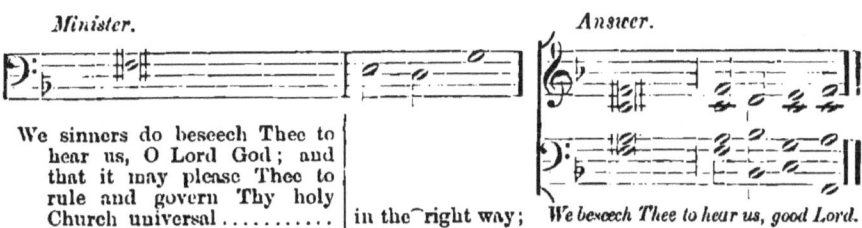

We sinners do beseech Thee to hear us, O Lord God; and that it may please Thee to rule and govern Thy holy Church universal .... | in the right way; *We beseech Thee to hear us, good Lord.*

That it may please Thee to bless and preserve all Christian Rulers and Magistrates, giving them grace to execute justice, and to | main-tain truth ;
We beseech Thee to hear us, good Lord.

That it may please Thee to illuminate all Bishops, Priests, and Deacons, with true knowledge and understanding of Thy Word; and that both by their preaching and living they may set it forth, and show | it ac-cordingly ;
We beseech Thee to hear us, good Lord.

That it may please Thee to bless and keep | all thy people ;
We beseech Thee to hear us, good Lord.

That it may please Thee to give to all nations unity, | peace, and concord ;
We beseech Thee to hear us, good Lord.

That it may please Thee to give us an heart to love and fear Thee, and diligently to live after | Thy com-mandments ; *We beseech Thee to hear us, good Lord.*

That it may please Thee to give to all Thy people increase of grace to hear meekly Thy Word, and to receive it with pure affection, and to bring forth the fruits | of the Spirit ; *We beseech Thee to hear us, good Lord.*

That it may please Thee to bring into the way of truth all such as have erred, and | are de-ceived ; *We beseech Thee to hear us, good Lord.*

That it may please Thee to strengthen such as do stand ; and to comfort and help the weak-hearted ; and to raise up those who fall; and finally to beat down Satan | un-der our feet ; *We beseech Thee to hear us, good Lord.*

That it may please Thee to succour, help, and comfort, all who are in danger, necessity, and | tribu-lation ; *We beseech Thee to hear us, good Lord.*

That it may please Thee to preserve all who travel by land or by water, all women in the perils of child-birth, all sick persons, and young children ; and to show thy pity upon all prison- | ers and captives ; *We beseech Thee to hear us, good Lord.*

That it may please Thee to defend, and provide for, the fatherless children, and widows, and all who are desolate | and op-pressed ; *We beseech Thee to hear us, good Lord.*

That it may please Thee to have mercy up- | on all men ;
We beseech Thee to hear us, good Lord.

That it may please Thee to forgive our enemies, persecutors, and slanderers, and to | turn their hearts ; *We beseech Thee to hear us, good Lord.*

That it may please Thee to give and preserve to our use the kindly fruits of the earth, so that in due time we | may en-joy them ; *We beseech Thee to hear us, good Lord.*

That it may please Thee to give us true repentance ; to forgive us all our sins, negligences, and ignorances ; and to endue us with the grace of Thy Holy Spirit to amend our lives according to thy | ho-ly Word ; *We beseech Thee to hear us, good Lord.*

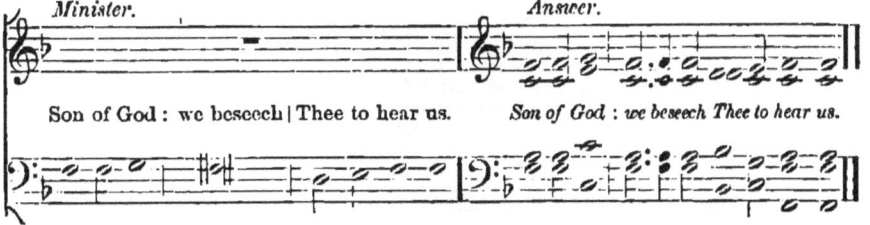

Son of God : we beseech | Thee to hear us.   Son of God : *we beseech Thee to hear us.*

The Litany. 73

Minister.
O Lord, deal not with us according to our sins.

Answer.
Neither reward us according to our in-i-qui-ties.

Minister.
Let us pray.

Minister.
O God, merciful Father, Who despisest not the sighing of a contrite heart, nor the desire of such as are sorrowful; Mercifully assist our prayers which we make before Thee in all our troubles and adversities, whensoever they oppress us; and graciously hear us, that those evils which the craft and subtilty of the devil or man worketh against us, may, by Thy good providence, be brought to nought; that we Thy servants, being hurt by no persecutions, may evermore give thanks unto Thee in Thy holy Church; through Jesus Christ our Lord.

Answer.
O Lord, arise, help us, and deliver us for Thy Name's sake.

Minister.
O God, we have heard with our ears, and our fathers have declared unto us, the noble works that Thou didst in their days, and in the old time be - - - - - - - - - fore them.

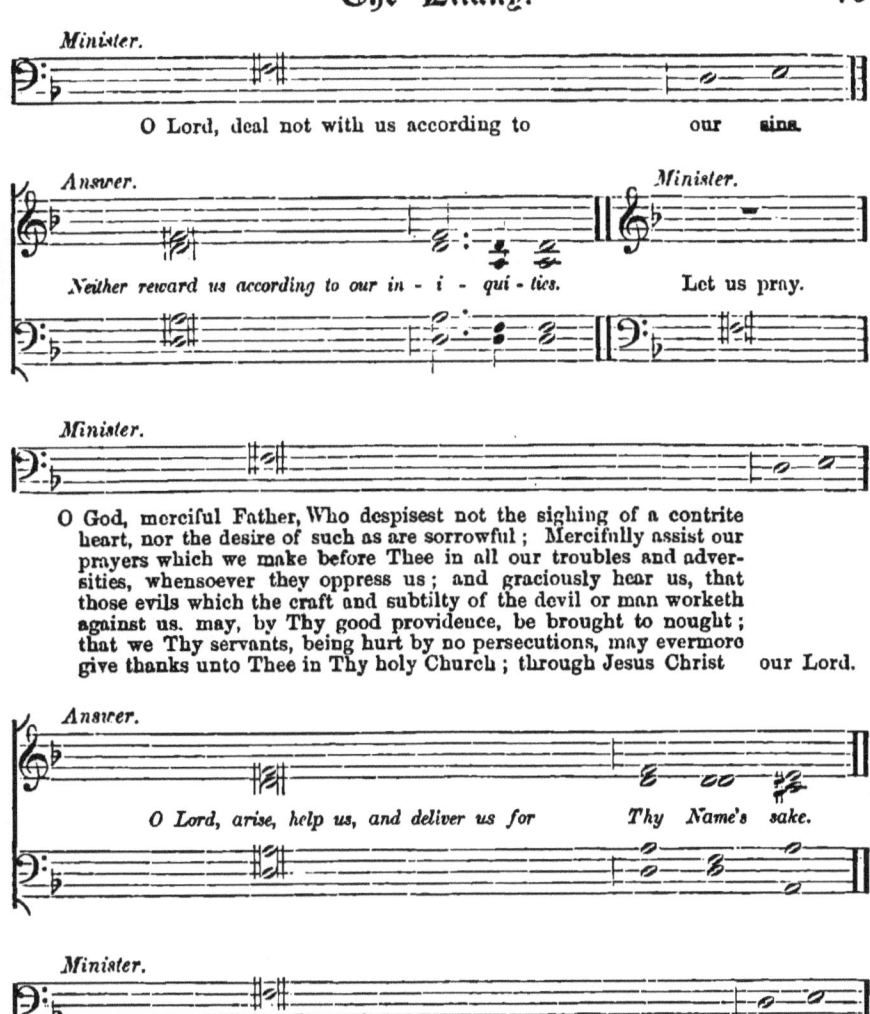

The Litany.

Minister.
Glory be to the Father, and to the Son, and to the Ho - ly Ghost;

Answer.
As it was in the beginning, is now, and ever shall be, world without end. A - men.

Minister.
From our enemies defend us, O Christ.

Answer.
Graciously look upon our af - flic-tions.

Minister.
With pity behold the sorrows of our hearts.

Answer.
Mercifully forgive the sins of Thy peo-ple.

Minister.
Favourably with mercy hear our prayers.

Answer.
O Son of David, have mercy up - on us.

Minister.
Both now and ever, vouchsafe to hear us, . . . O Christ.

Answer.
Graciously hear us, O Christ; graciously hear us, O Lord Christ.

The Litany.

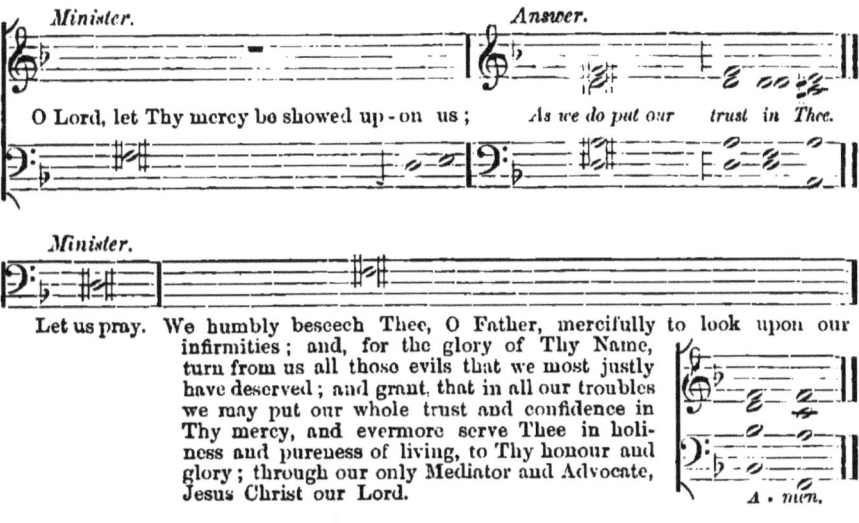

Let us pray. We humbly beseech Thee, O Father, mercifully to look upon our infirmities; and, for the glory of Thy Name, turn from us all those evils that we most justly have deserved; and grant, that in all our troubles we may put our whole trust and confidence in Thy mercy, and evermore serve Thee in holiness and pureness of living, to Thy honour and glory; through our only Mediator and Advocate, Jesus Christ our Lord. *A - men.*

A General Thanksgiving.

ALMIGHTY God, Father of all mercies, we, Thine unworthy servants, do give Thee most humble and hearty thanks for all Thy goodness and loving-kindness to us, and to all men. We bless Thee for our creation, preservation, and all the blessings of this life; but, above all, for Thine inestimable love in the redemption of the world by our Lord Jesus Christ; for the means of grace, and for the hope of glory. And, we beseech Thee, give us that due sense of all Thy mercies, that our hearts may be unfeignedly thankful, and that we may show forth Thy praise, not only with our lips, but in our lives; by giving up ourselves to Thy service, and by walking before Thee in holiness and righteousness all our days; through Jesus Christ our Lord, to whom, with Thee and the Holy Ghost, be all honour and glory, world without end.  *A - men.*

A Prayer of St. Chrysostom.

ALMIGHTY God, Who hast given us grace at this time with one accord to make our common supplications unto Thee; and dost promise that when two or three are gathered together in Thy Name Thou wilt grant their requests; Fulfil now, O Lord, the desires and petitions of Thy servants, as may be most expedient for them; granting us in this world knowledge of Thy truth, and in the world to come life everlasting.  *A - men.*

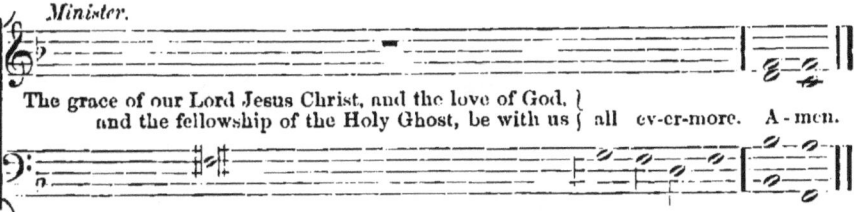

The grace of our Lord Jesus Christ, and the love of God, and the fellowship of the Holy Ghost, be with us all ev-er-more. A-men.

HERE ENDETH THE LITANY.

Holy Communion.

166.   Kyrie eleison.   W. H. WALTER.

1–9. Lord, have mercy upon us, and incline our hearts to . . keep this law.
10. Lord, have mercy upon us, and write all these Thy laws in our hearts, we beseech . . Thee.

167.   PLAIN SONG.

After 9 Commandments.

Lord, have mer-cy up-on us, and incline our hearts to keep this law.

After the 10th Commandment.

and write all these Thy laws in our hearts, we be-seech Thee.

168.   GOUNOD.

After 9 Commandments.

Lord, have mer-cy up-on us, and incline our hearts to keep this law.

After the 10th Commandment.   *Più lento.*

us, and write all these Thy laws in our hearts, we be-seech Thee.

Holy Communion.

169. *From BEETHOVEN.*

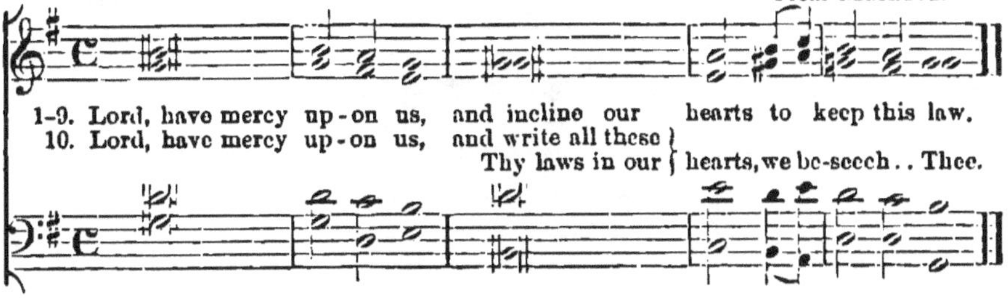

1-9. Lord, have mercy up-on us, and incline our hearts to keep this law.
10. Lord, have mercy up-on us, and write all these Thy laws in our hearts, we be-seech.. Thee.

170. *DR. NARES.*

After 9 Commandments.
Lord, have mer-cy up-on us, and in-cline our hearts to keep this law.

After the 10th Commandment. *Slower.*
us, and write all these Thy laws in our hearts, we be-seech Thee.

171. *OTIS R. GREENE.*

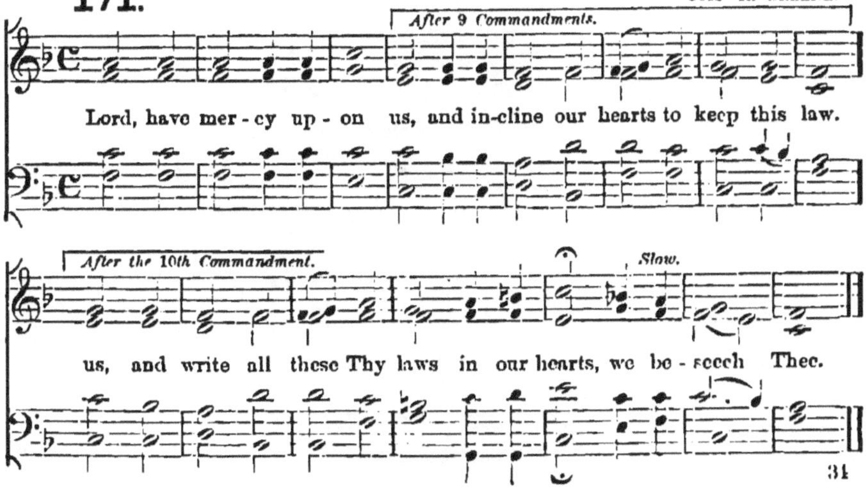

After 9 Commandments.
Lord, have mer-cy up-on us, and in-cline our hearts to keep this law.

After the 10th Commandment. *Slow.*
us, and write all these Thy laws in our hearts, we be-seech Thee.

Holy Communion.

Holy Communion.

186. "Godliness is great riches." — J. Barnby.

Godliness is great riches, if a man be content with that he hath: for we brought nothing .·. in-to this world, neither may we car-ry a - ny-thing out.

187. "Be merciful after thy power." — J. Barnby.

Be mer-ci - ful af - ter thy power. If thou hast much, give plenteous - ly; if thou hast lit-tle, do thy dil - i-gence gladly to give of that lit-tle, for so, so, gath'rest thou thy - self a good reward in the day of ne-ces-si - ty.

Holy Communion.

191. Sursum corda. **192.**

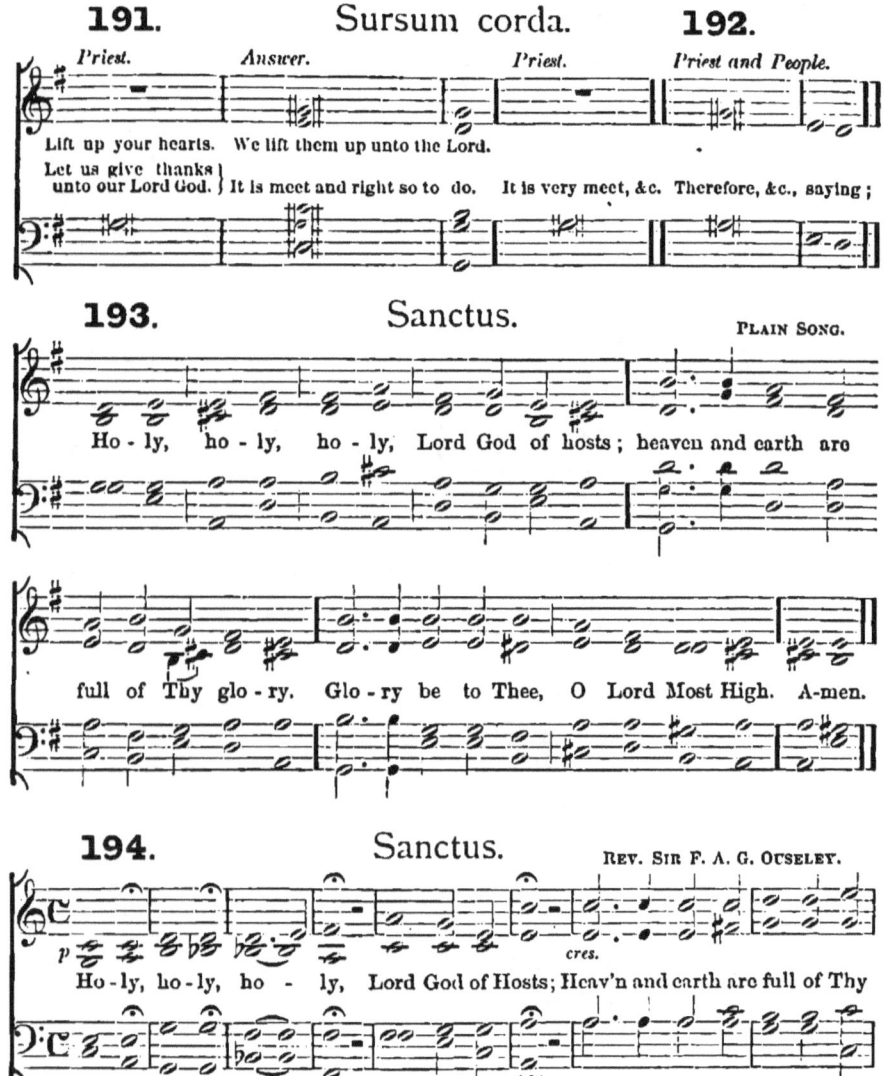

Priest. Lift up your hearts.
Answer. We lift them up unto the Lord.
Priest. Let us give thanks unto our Lord God. } It is meet and right so to do.
Priest and People. It is very meet, &c. Therefore, &c., saying;

193. Sanctus. PLAIN SONG.

Ho-ly, ho-ly, ho-ly, Lord God of hosts; heaven and earth are full of Thy glo-ry. Glo-ry be to Thee, O Lord Most High. A-men.

194. Sanctus. REV. SIR F. A. G. OUSELEY.

Ho-ly, ho-ly, ho - ly, Lord God of Hosts; Heav'n and earth are full of Thy

Holy Communion.

197. Sursum corda. N. B. WARREN.

Lift up your hearts.   We lift them up un-to the Lord
Let us give thanks unto our Lord God. It is meet and right (*Omit* . . .) so to do.

It is very meet, &c.

198. Trisagion.

Moderato.

There-fore with An-gels and Arch-an-gels, and with all the com-pa-ny of

heaven, we laud and mag-ni-fy Thy glo-ri-ous Name, ev-er-more praising Thee, and

saying, Ho-ly, ho-ly, ho-ly Lord God of Hosts; Heav'n and earth are full of

Holy Communion.

200.   Gloria in excelsis.   OLD CHANT.

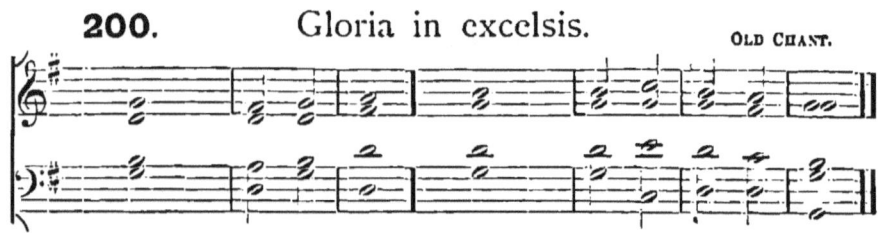

Glory **be** to | God · on | high : ‖ and on **earth** | peace, · good- | will · towards | men.

We praise Thee, we bless **Thee,** we | wor-ship | Thee : ‖ we glorify Thee, we give **thanks** to | Thee · for | Thy · great | glory.

O Lord **God,** | heaven-ly | King : ‖ **God** the | Fa-ther | Al- = | mighty.
O Lord, the only-begotten **Son** | Je - sus | Christ : ‖ O Lord God, Lamb of **God,** | Son · = | of · the | Father.

That takest **away** the | sins · of ͟ the | world : ‖ have **mercy** up- | on · = | us.
Thou that takest **away** the | sins · of ͟ the | world: ‖ have **mercy** up- | on · = | us.
Thou that takest **away** the | sins · of ͟ the | world : ‖ **re-** | ceive · our | prayer.
Thou that sittest at the right **hand** of | God · the | Father : ‖ have **mercy** up- | on · = | us.

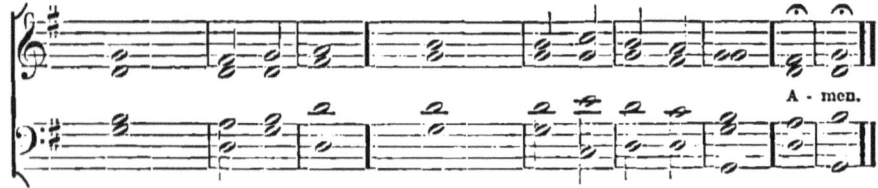

For Thou **ônly** | art · = | holy : ‖ **Thou** | on - ly | art · the | Lord.
Thou only, O **Christ,** with the | Ho - ly | Ghost : ‖ art most **high in** the | glory · of | God · the | Father. ‖ A- | men.

INDEX.

Morning Prayer.

VENITE.

SINGLE CHANTS.	Key.	Page.	No.
Tallis	F	3	1
Sir John Goss	F	3	2
Goodson	C	3	3
Dr. W. Hayes	A	4	4
Farrant	F	4	5
Bishop Turton	A♭	4	6

DOUBLE CHANTS.

J Robinson | F♯ | 5 | 7
Rev. W. H. Havergal | E | 5 | 8
Dr. W. Boyce | D | 5 | 9
J. Turle | F | 5 | 10
R. Langdon | F | 5 | 11

GREGORIAN TONES.

VIII. 1 | A | 43 | 104
VIII. 2 | A | 43 | 105
V. 1 | D | 43 | 106
I. 4 | F | 44 | 107
III. 3 | G | 44 | 108
VII. 4 | G | 44 | 109
I. 1 | F | 45 | 110
I. 8 | F | 45 | 111
V. 5 (*Rouen Med.*) | D | 45 | 112

TE DEUM LAUDAMUS.
DOUBLE CHANTS.

Gibbons | F♯ | 6 | 12
Dr. Hodges | A♭ | 7 | 13
J. Turle | C | 7 | 14
Anon | C | 7 | 15
Anon | C min | 7 | 16
W. H. Walter | D | 7 | 17
Frederick Helmore | D | 8 | 18
(Irregular) | F | 10 | 19

GREGORIAN TONES.

VIII. 1 (*Rouen Med.*) | B♭ | 46 | 113
VIII. 2 (*Rouen Med.*) | B♭ | 46 | 114
VI. 1 | G | 46 | 115
V. 3 (*Rouen Med.*) | D | 46 | 116
V. 1 (*Rouen Med.*) | D | 46 | 117

TE DEUM. (Congregational.)
J. H. Cornell | F | 11 | 20

BENEDICITE.
DOUBLE CHANTS.

W. H. Walter | B♭ | 16 | 21
Dr. W. Hayes | F | 16 | 22
Rev. W. H. Havergal | C | 16 | 23
J. H. Cornell | G | 18 | 24

GREGORIAN TONES.

V. 5 (*Rouen Med.*) | D | 48 | 118
III. 4 | A | 48 | 119
V. 1 | D | 48 | 120

JUBILATE DEO.
SINGLE CHANTS.

Sir G. J. Elvey | B♭ | 20 | 25
Charles King | F | 20 | 26
Dean Aldrich | A | 20 | 27
Dr. W. Hayes | D | 20 | 28
V. Novello | A | 20 | 29

DOUBLE CHANTS.

J. H. Cornell | E | 21 | 30
W. H. Walter | B♭ | 21 | 31
Dr. J. S. Smith | B♭ | 21 | 32
Dean Aldrich | F | 21 | 33

GREGORIAN TONES.

II. 2 (*Rouen Med.*) | G | 50 | 121
VI. 2 | F | 50 | 122
IV. 2 | D | 50 | 123
IV. 1 | A | 50 | 124

BENEDICTUS.
SINGLE CHANTS.	Key.	Page.	No.
Rev. Sir F. A. G. Ouseley	B♭	22	34
Dr. Crotch	A	22	35
Dr. W. Hayes	C	22	36
V. Novello	B♭	22	37
W. Hine	G	22	38

DOUBLE CHANTS.

C. Clarke | F | 23 | 39
B. Lawes | B♭ | 23 | 40
Dr. Hodges | F | 23 | 41
Dr. Worgan | B♭ | 23 | 42

GREGORIAN TONES.

I. 2 | F | 51 | 125
VII. 1 | G | 51 | 126
III. 1 | A | 51 | 127
Tonus Regius | F | 51 | 128

Evening Prayer.

CANTATE DOMINO.
SINGLE CHANTS.

W. Russell | F | 24 | 43
Sir John Goss | A | 24 | 44
Rev. W. Felton | F | 24 | 45
V. Novello | A | 24 | 46
A. B. Reinagle | E | 24 | 47

DOUBLE CHANTS.

Dr. Randall | E | 25 | 48
Lord Mornington | D | 25 | 49
T. Attwood | C | 25 | 50

GREGORIAN TONES.

I. 6 | F | 52 | 129
III. 1 | A | 52 | 130
V. 2 (*Rouen Med.*) | D | 52 | 131

BONUM EST CONFITERI.
SINGLE CHANTS.

Dr. Woodward | C | 26 | 51
Dr. Hayes | E | 26 | 52
J. Travers | F♯ | 26 | 53
W. H. Monk | F | 26 | 54
W. Hine | G min | 26 | 55

DOUBLE CHANTS.

J. Soaper (*Altered from*) | D | 27 | 56
Handel (*Arr. from*) | F | 27 | 57
Dr. Dupuis | F | 27 | 58
J. Turle | F | 27 | 59

GREGORIAN TONES.

VIII. 1 | A | 53 | 132
VIII. 2 | A | 53 | 133
V. 1 | D | 53 | 134
V. 3 | D | 53 | 135

DEUS MISEREATUR.
SINGLE CHANTS.

Dr. Turner | A | 28 | 60
Dr. Aldrich | G | 28 | 61
J. Barnby | F♯ | 28 | 62
Sir G. J. Elvey | B♭ | 28 | 63
W. H. Walter | B♭ | 28 | 64

DOUBLE CHANTS.

J. H. Cornell | F♯ | 29 | 65
W. Hawes | B♭ | 29 | 66
T. Attwood | E | 29 | 67

GREGORIAN TONES.

I. 1 | F | 54 | 136
I. 6 | F | 54 | 137
V. 5 (*Rouen Med.*) | D | 54 | 138
VII. 1 | G | 55 | 139
VII. 3 | E min | 55 | 140
Tonus Peregrinus | F | 55 | 141

INDEX.

BENEDIC. ANIMA MEA.
SINGLE CHANTS.
	Key	Page	No.
W. Lee	F	30	68
E. J. Hopkins	E♭	30	69
E. G. Monk	C	30	70
W. Dyce	G	30	71
Dr. B. Cooke	F	30	72

DOUBLE CHANTS.
	Key	Page	No.
Dr. Barrow	F	31	73
T. Norris	A	31	74
Dr. B. Cooke	G	31	75

GREGORIAN TONES.
	Key	Page	No.
I. 2	F	56	142
VII. 1	G	56	143
III. 2	A	56	144

Occasional Anthems.

EASTER DAY.
SINGLE CHANTS.
	Key	Page	No.
Dr. J. Nares	A	32	76
E. G. Monk	A	32	77
Rev. Sir F. A. G. Ouseley	A	32	78
J. Travers	F♯	32	79
W. Savage	C	32	80

DOUBLE CHANTS.
	Key	Page	No.
Lord Mornington	F♯	33	81
Anon	E	33	82
E. Higgins	F	33	83

GREGORIAN TONES.
	Key	Page	No.
VIII. 1	A	57	145
VIII. 2	A	57	146
V. 3	D	57	147

THANKSGIVING DAY.
SINGLE CHANTS.
	Key	Page	No.
Dr. W. Hayes	F	34	84
Dr. Rimbault	F	34	85
Rev. Sir F. A. G. Ouseley	E	34	86

GREGORIAN TONES.
	Key	Page	No.
VIII. 1	A	58	148
VIII. 2	A	58	149
V. 3	D	58	150

INSTITUTION OF MINISTERS.
SINGLE CHANTS.
	Key	Page	No.
T. Purcell	G	35	87
Dr. Alcock	G	35	88

GREGORIAN TONES. (See Thanksgiving Day.)

CONSECRATION OF CHURCHES.
SINGLE CHANTS.
	Key	Page	No.
Farrant	F	36	89
P. Humphrey	E♭	36	90
Old Scotch Chant	G	36	91

GREGORIAN TONES. (See Thanksgiving Day.)

MISERERE MEI, DEUS.
	Key	Page	No.
J. H. Cornell	E min	37	92

MAGNIFICAT.
SINGLE CHANTS.
	Key	Page	No.
Anon	D♭	40	98
Anon	F	40	99
W. H. Walter	F	40	100
J. Jones	D♭	40	101
J. Barnby	B min	40	102
P. Fussell	G	41	103

GREGORIAN TONES.
	Key	Page	No.
I. 1	F	60	151
V. 5 (Rouen Med.)	D	60	152
III. 4	B♭	60	153

NUNC DIMITTIS.
SINGLE CHANTS. (See Magnificat.)
GREGORIAN TONES.
	Key	Page	No.
I. 2	F	61	154
III. 3	D♭	61	155
VII. 4	G	61	156
Tonus Regius	F	61	157

Burial of the Dead.
SINGLE CHANTS.
	Key	Page	No.
Rev. W. Felton	E♭	38	93
Dr. Crotch	D min	38	94
Farrant	G min	38	95

DOUBLE CHANTS.
	Key	Page	No.
T. Morley	D min	39	96
Rev. J. Flintoft	E min	39	97

Burial Service. W. H. WALTER.
	Key	Page	No.
Opening Sentences	E♭	62	158
Burial Psalm	E♭	63	159
Burial Anthems	E♭	64	160
"I heard a voice."	E♭	65	161
"I heard a voice." (Redhead)	C	65	162
De Profundis	C	66	163

Choral Service.
	Page	No.
Preces and Responses	67	164
The Apostles' Creed	68	

The Litany.
	Key	Page	No.
	F	70	165

Holy Communion.
KYRIE ELEISON.
	Key	Page	No.
W. H. Walter (chant)	F	76	166
Plain Song	F	76	167
Gounod	G	76	168
Beethoven (chant)	G	77	169
Dr. Nares	F	77	170
Otis R. Greene	F	77	171
Rev. Sir F. A. G. Ouseley	C	78	172
Sir G. J. Elvey	D	78	173
N. B. Warren	A	79	174

GLORIA TIBI.
	Page	No.
N. B. Warren	79	175
W. W. R.	79	176
Plain Song	79	177
Gounod	79	178
T. Tallis	79	179
W. H. Walter	79	180

ASCRIPTION (After Sermon).
	Key	Page	No.
J. H. Cornell	F♯	80	181

GLORIA PATRI.
	Key	Page	No.
Dr. Nares	D	80	182

OFFERTORY.
	Page	No.
"Blessed be Thou." (v. 5.)	81	183
"Let your light." W. H. Monk	81	184
"While we have time." J. Barnby	81	185
"Godliness is great riches." do.	82	186
"Be merciful." do.	82	187
"Give alms." do.	83	188
"Blessed is the man." do.	83	189
"Blessed is he." (vii. 4.)	83	190

SURSUM CORDA.
	Key	Page	No.
Plain Song	G	84	191
N. B. Warren	A	86	197
Trisagion	G	84	192

SANCTUS.
	Key	Page	No.
Plain Song	G	84	193
Sir F. A. G. Ouseley	C	84	194
A. S. Cooper	D	85	195
Sir G. J. Elvey	A	85	196
N. B. Warren	A	86	198

GLORIA IN EXCELSIS.
	Key	Page	No.
J. H. Cornell	F	87	199
Old Chant	G	90	200

www.ingramcontent.com/pod-product-compliance
Lightning Source LLC
Chambersburg PA
CBHW020255090426
42735CB00009B/1096